IMAGES
of America

HAVERHILL'S IMMIGRANTS

AT THE TURN OF THE CENTURY

A POLISH WEDDING. Andrzej Bizeur (1892–1962) and Anna Klecha (1893–1987) celebrated their marriage in the second decade of the 20th century in their new home—Haverhill. They surrounded themselves with their fellow immigrants. From left to right are as follows: (seated) Katherine (Bizeur) Rowinski, Anna and Andrzej, and Anthony Sudol with his daughter Katherine; (standing) Tekla Wos, John Wyka, Mary (Bayek) Januszewski, and Joseph Klecha.

COVER: GREEKS IN COSTUMES. Unidentified Greek actors and musicians, many with the classic *bouzoukis*, step out into the alleyway for a breath of fresh air. The Greeks were the last of the six immigrant groups described in this book to come to Haverhill.

IMAGES
of America

HAVERHILL'S
IMMIGRANTS
AT THE TURN OF THE CENTURY

Patricia Trainor O'Malley

ARCADIA

Published by Arcadia Publishing,
an imprint of Tempus Publishing, Inc.
2 Cumberland Street
Charleston, SC 29401

Printed in Great Britain.

Library of Congress Catalog Card Number applied for.

For all general information contact Arcadia Publishing at:
Telephone 843-853-2070
Fax 843-853-0044
E-Mail edit@arcadiaimages.com

For customer service and orders:
Toll-Free 1-888-313-BOOK

Visit us on the internet at http://www.arcadiaimages.com

In memory of Lenora Marie (Donovan) Trainor (1903–1999). Rest in Peace.

AUGUST CARBONE'S STORE. Each of Haverhill's immigrant groups in the early 20th century had individuals who opened grocery stores, not just for their own ethnic group but for everyone in the neighborhood. August Carbone's store was on Water Street just beyond the Route 125 bridge over the Merrimack River. The store was in operation until urban renewal cleared that whole corner and replaced it with the One Water Street senior citizen housing.

CONTENTS

DINA DESCOTEAUX. Dina came from French-Canadian stock, one of the largest immigrant groups in Haverhill in the early 20th century. She was the eldest child of Olivier and Marie Louise Decoteaux and was born in Lewiston, ME, soon after her parents had moved there from Canada. The family moved to Haverhill when was Dina was 15, and she went to work in the local shoe shops. Dina died in 1940.

INTRODUCTION

In 1997, we published a photographic history of turn-of-the-century Haverhill. That volume focused on the buildings and landscapes of the growing industrial site as it was transformed from a town of 5,000 to a city of 50,000. We attempted to show the impact of the booming shoe industry not only on the city's growth, but also on its physical appearance, its architectural styles, and its changing streetscapes. The book included chapters on Haverhill's thriving mercantile "downtown" and the city's response to the demand for more and improved public services.

When individuals were portrayed, they were from the "Yankee," or Anglo-Saxon, part of the population. This was done purposefully, for already in the planning stage were photographic histories on Haverhill's newer immigrant groups. The first of these, *The Irish in Haverhill, Massachusetts,* arrived in the bookstores on Saint Patrick's Day, 1998. So great was the response to that ethnic overview, and so many were the offers of additional photographs, that a second volume on the Irish was completed and made available to the public by Saint Patrick's Day, 1999.

So now we offer this look, and it is no more than a quick glance, at some of the other immigrant groups that had settled into Haverhill by the beginning of the 20th century. Limitations of space restricted the number of groups that could be covered to six: French Canadians, Italians, Armenians, Lithuanians, Poles, and Greeks. Conspicuously missing from this volume are the Central and Eastern European Jewish immigrants, and the African American migrants from the American South, who were contemporaries of the people selected. All we can offer in defense is that these groups have not been totally neglected. Bertha Woodman's *From the Hill to Main Street* has chronicled the story of Haverhill's Jewish community, and the Haverhill Historical Society has an on-going project of recording the narrative of the African Americans in the city.

One chapter each is hardly sufficient to tell the story of the six groups chosen for this volume. At best, we have tried to tell a common story of immigration to Haverhill, a common story of employment in the shoe shops, and a common story of the ways that each group tried to maintain its distinctive culture and traditions while assimilating into American society.

Some of these people fled persecution and cut all ties with their homeland. Some came to Haverhill for economic reasons and, after saving enough money, returned to their birthplace to buy a farm, or a store, or to send younger relatives to take their place in America. Some, like the French Canadians, were only a train ride away from their native places, and could make regular visits to family and friends. Each story is somewhat the same, and yet a bit different.

Very few of these photographs have come from public archives. Almost all have come from private collections and this book would not have been possible without the cooperation of dozens of people who willingly, and sometimes cautiously, offered their family treasures to us. Many pictures were handed over with the warning, "Be very careful! This is the only photograph we have of Grandmother/Grandfather/Mother/Father." For many, it was an act of faith to part, even temporarily, with their prizes and hand them over to a comparative stranger. We hope this volume justifies their willingness to cooperate. We know that the greater community will be the beneficiary for this opportunity to look into the past and freeze in time the faces of *Haverhill's Immigrants in the Early 20th Century*.

ACKNOWLEDGMENTS

The following have contributed photographs and information used in this volume. The book was impossible without their contributions. Many thanks to: All Saints Parish, Aldona and Joe Belsky, Michael Buglione, Rita Carbone Cappabianca, Donna Carbone, Verna Carbone, Vicky Collins, Janet and Dick Daly, Kathy Carbone Daly, Connie Montebianchi Fiala, Ellen and John Gallant, Robert Gardella, Heather and David Goudsward, Vahe Gulezian, Dora Gardella Hansbury, the Haverhill Historical Society, the Haverhill Public Library, Sara Jaffarian, Paul and Margaret Kazarosian, John and Victoria Kmiec, Vaughan Kochakian, Gail Kolizeras, Sophie Kosciewicz, Kara Kosmes, Claire Lavallee, Edolo Lupi, Al and Charlotte Movsesian, Virginia Nazaretian, Dr. Frank A. Oberti III, Ann Paolino, M. Patricia Perrault, Mary Zoukis Papastravos, Foula Peterson, Matthew Poth, Carmen Proulx, Jim and Kathy Rurak, Joanne Rurak, Fred Scamporino, Mary Anuszewski Sheehan, Norman Taupeka, the Tavitian Family, Algerd Truska, Georgia and John Valhouli, Mary Ann Valhouli, Peter and Joan Vlahos, Jeanette Warchol, Mary Wezowicz, Robert Wysocki, and John Ziminski.

One

THE FRENCH CANADIANS

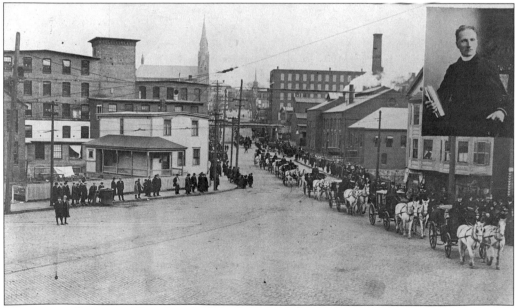

LAFAYETTE SQUARE. The French-Canadian community in Haverhill radiated out from Lafayette Square by Little River. Its first church was to the east of the square on Grand Street. The major function hall for the Franco community was in the St. Jean Baptiste building in the square. The first school building, for boys, was immediately west of this area. This December 1914 picture shows the funeral procession for Fr. Alexandre Loudes S.M., assistant rector of the parish. A native of France, Fr. Loudes (insert) had served at St. Joseph's from 1902 until 1914 when, at age 61, he died of pneumonia. The funeral procession proceeded from the church on Walnut Street, down Winter Street, to Lafayette Square on its way to St. Joseph's Cemetery, where Fr. Loudes was interred.

CHARLES SAVIGNAC'S BRICKYARD. The first French Canadians in Haverhill appear on the 1850 census. The majority of them were brick makers who boarded with Yankee families in the city's North Parish and in Plaistow, NH, where the clay pits were located. Charles Savignac immigrated from Quebec in 1859, learned the art of brick making, and soon owned one of the largest works in the area. This is a view of the clay mixing bin. The man on the left is thought to be Savignac's son Frank.

PHILIP LeBLANC'S FLOAT. Haverhill celebrated the 250th anniversary of its founding in 1890. An enormous parade was held with countless floats. This float, with its miniature house, was sponsored by Philip LeBlanc, carpenter. According to his illustrated advertisement in the 1891 City Directory, LeBlanc was also a contractor, real estate agent, and trucker. He also sold sand! His home and business were on Hilldale Avenue "opposite the cemetery." His name disappears from the directories after 1892.

OLIVIER AND MARIE LOUISE DECOTEAUX. Olivier Decoteaux (1837–1924) was born in Canada and married Marie Louise Marcotte (1845–1932) in Danville, Canada, in 1867. They lived in Lewiston, ME, before moving to Haverhill in 1895. Olivier was a blacksmith. Marie Louise and Olivier had ten children. Three of the seven surviving children are, from left to right, Dina (1870–1940), Aime (1877–1962), and Imelda (1886–1954). The family home was at 103 Bellevue Avenue

MARIE LOUISE DESCOTEAUX. Louise, born in 1868, was the oldest of the Descoteaux children. In 1891 she married Adolphus Perrrault in Lewiston, ME, and moved to his home in Haverhill. Like her mother, Louise had ten children, seven of whom survived childhood. The Perraults lived on Eudora Street near Hilldale Avenue. Louise died in Haverhill in 1919. She is shown wearing her First Communion outfit about 1878.

ADOLPHUS PERRAULT AND FAMILY. Adophus was born in Quebec. He first appears in the Haverhill 1889 City Directory, where he is listed as a shoemaker. After marrying Louise Descoteaux and moving to Eudora Street, he became a house painter. Adolphus died in Haverhill in 1936. He is shown with his seven surviving children. They are as follows, from left to right: (front row) Joseph (born 1903) and Albert (born 1904); (back row) Oscar (born 1896), Imelda (born 1892), Isabella (born 1900), Adolphus, Lucina (born 1899), and Laura (born 1895).

PATRIOTIC LITTLE ALBERT. Albert was the youngest of Adolphus and Louise Perrault's children. He was born in 1904 and was a teenager when his mother died. This photograph is dated September 5, 1909, which would suggest that Albert is dressed for a Labor Day celebration. His huge baker's hat is just the right topping for a festive occasion. Albert married Mary Ellen Lowes in 1940. They had four children –Mary Patricia, Jean, Albert William, and Raymond. Albert died in 1989, Mary Ellen in 1969.

NAPOLEON THERIAULT, SUCCESS STORY. Theriault was born in Montreal, Quebec, in 1876 and moved with his family to Haverhill in 1881. Napoleon's father was a shoemaker, and after completing public school, young Theriault joined him in the factory. He learned all aspects of the trade and became associated with a new firm, Witherell & Dobbins. Theriault became vice president of the firm, which was one of Haverhill's most successful during the 1920s. He married fellow Canadian Albertine DeCoteau (1878–1961), daughter of Edward, in 1901. She had immigrated when an infant. The Theriault home was at 322 Broadway. Napoleon and Albertine had four children—Raoul, Irene, Edgar, and Paul. The two youngest were still in school when Napoleon died at age 46, in 1924.

THE GAUVIN FAMILY OF SARGENT SQUARE. Jean Baptiste Gauvin was born in Canada in 1840. When a young man, he moved to Haverhill where, in 1870, he married Lucinda Dauphinais Finney. Her father, Peter, was a shoemaker with a home in Sargent's Square. Lucinda was born in Haverhill in 1850—thus the Finneys were one of the pioneering Franco families. Jean Baptiste was a shoemaker. He eventually moved his family into his father-in-law's house, a small gambrel-roofed building in Sargent Square, later renumbered 99 Lafayette Square. Lucinda bore ten children, seven of whom survived childhood. This picture dates from about 1894, soon after baby Delvina had died. From left to right are as follows: (front row) Achille (1880–1962, never married), Mary Jane (1888–1904), Lucinda (1850–1946), Emma (1886–1987, married Hormidas DesFosses), Agnes (1884–1973, married Ira Pullen), Jean Baptiste (1840–1914), and Pierre (1878–1958, never married); (back row) Camille (1874–1946, married Malvina Hamelin), Virginia (1873–1962, married Ernest Brouillette), and John Baptist Jr. (1877–1972, never married).

THE C.K. FOX STITCHING ROOM. Haverhill's great attraction for French Canadians, as for all its late-19th-century immigrant groups, was its shoe industry. Not only the shoe shops, but all the auxiliary industries that grew up with them, guaranteed regular, though seasonal, employment. Because the shoe industry was not dominated by any one major corporation, the failure of one company would not necessarily affect the entire industry in the city, as happened in textile manufacturing locales. The C.K. Fox Stitching Co. was located on Duncan Street, near Winter Street. Two women in this picture have been identified. Helene Boiselle is at a sewing machine (second from the left). She married Joseph Rousseau. Valeda Gaurone, who married Sabine Fecteau, is also at a sewing machine (fourth from the left).

THE ROY HOUSEHOLD.
Edward A. Roy (1868–1951, standing at left in his shirt sleeves) was a shoe pattern maker. He lived with his family in this Victorian-style house at 468 Hilldale Avenue, at the corner of Edmund Street. Next to Roy is his father-in-law, Azarie Poirier, a laster in a shoe shop. In the front, from left to right, are Roy's wife, Parmelia (1874–1963), and three of their children—Lillian, Adolph (1895–1980), and Antoinette.

THE COMEAUS OF NOVA SCOTIA. Etienne ("Steve") Comeau (1880–1962) and his sister Philomene (1883–1958) were born in Grosses Coques, Nova Scotia. Steve had a plumbing business in Sargent Square. In 1906, he married Evangeline Deveau (1880–1945), who was born in Meteghan, Nova Scotia. They had eight children. Steve's arm was crushed when a stove fell on it. He was able to return to work, but never had full use of the arm again. His sister Philomene came to Haverhill as a domestic for a family that wanted their children to speak French. They would not allow her to learn English while she lived in their house. The English she spoke in later years was overlaid with a thick accent as a result.

FERDINAND THIBODEAU OF NOVA SCOTIA. "Fred" Thibodeau was born in 1886 in Meteghan, Digby County, Nova Scotia. His father sailed cargo ships between Nova Scotia and the Caribbean. After experiencing one particularly ferocious storm while sailing with his father, Fred vowed to never sail again. He turned to carpentry, which he had learned from the shipbuilders in his home town. Fred first appeared in the Haverhill 1906 City Directory, living in the same boardinghouse as Steve Comeau. Perhaps this is how he met Steve's sister Philomene. For many years Fred was employed by the Killam Construction Co.

A SUMMER VISIT TO CANADA. A common feature to the experiences of many Canadian immigrants—French as well as Irish—were annual trips back to the home farm to help-out at haying season. Transportation to Quebec or the Maritime Provinces was accessible and relatively inexpensive. The seasonality of Haverhill's shoe industry, with its regular summer shutdowns, made such visits possible without jeopardizing employment. Here, Fred Thibodeau sits in a freshly cut hay field at his family home in Nova Scotia.

FERDINAND AND PHILOMENE THIBODEAU. The Thibodeaus, who married in 1909, had nine children, but only four survived childhood. They also cared for Fred's niece after his sister died. The Thibodeau home at 44 Hillside Street was a temporary home for many Nova Scotian immigrants. Some stayed only a few weeks, others for many months until regular employment could be found. Fred died suddenly of pneumonia in 1930 at the age of 44. Philomene survived Fred by 28 years. She died of cerebral meningitis while visiting her daughter in Newburyport at the age of 75.

VACATION TIME. By the early 20th century, it became more and more affordable for working-class families to take a vacation. Nearby places like Salisbury Beach, Country Pond, and Lake Attitash quickly became built up with simple cottages. In this photograph, recently married Fred (front left) and Philomene (standing, in the white dress in the center) Thibodeau vacation at the "Elmer Cottage" with relatives. The location is probably Lake Attitash, Amesbury, MA.

THREE GENERATIONS AT HAMPTON BEACH. Eliza Stone King (born in 1858), her daughter, Nora King Benoit (born in Haverhill in 1896), and Nora's nephew, William Leo King (born in Haverhill in 1910), spend a cooling day at the beach. Eliza came provided with a folding chair and returned with a box of salt water taffy. A good day all around!

LOUISE AND LIZA. Eliza Lapierre/Stone (right) was born near Montreal in 1858, the oldest of ten children of Andrew and Julia Lapierre. The family moved to Ticonderoga, NY. Liza married Judd Roy/King from Vermont and they lived in Haverhill by the mid-1890s. Louise A. Payette (left) was born in 1892 in Haverhill, one of 12 children. She left school before finishing her course and went to work in the shoe shops as a top stitcher. On Thanksgiving Day, 1915, she married George Raymond King, second son of Judd and Liza. They had three children. The family lived on Albert Street, just around the corner from his parents' home on Hilldale Avenue. Raymond King died in 1958. Louise lived another 30 years, keeping active in church activities and with needlework. She never learned to drive a car and walked for exercise. The regimen allowed her to live to the incredible age of 106. She was honored as the city's oldest resident when she died in 1998.

LOUISE ANNA THERIEN KING. Louise (right), wearing an extraordinary hat, was born in Canada in 1891. She married Joseph Leo King, son of Eliza and Judd King, in 1910, and is shown with her son, William Leo, and her husband's niece, Lucille Benoit, who was born in 1921. Lucille married Louis Thibodeau, son of Ferdinand and Philomene. Joseph King, Louise Anna's husband, died in 1958. Louise died in 1978. William Leo, who cared for his mother, died in 1986.

LAPIERRE/STONE GATHERINE. Judd and Eliza Lapierre King celebrated their 50th wedding anniversary in 1937. Six of Eliza's seven surviving siblings joined them in Haverhill for the celebration. Some had kept the French version of their name and the others had Anglicized it. They are, from left to right, as follows: (front row) Judd and Eliza; (back row) Clarinda "Lindy" Stone Beaudoin (born 1869), Emma Stone (born 1875, died in Haverhill in 1963), Joseph Lapierre (born 1864), Josephine "Phine" Stone (born 1873, died in Haverhill in 1956), Andrew Lapierre Jr. (born 1868), and Mary Lapierre Abare (born 1861). Judd worked at various positions in local shoe shops until injured in an auto accident, after which he operated a small grocery store at 441 Hilldale Avenue, opposite the family home at 458 Hilldale Avenue.

THE LaPIERRES OF QUEBEC. Adelard LaPierre and his wife, Valerie Brochu, were both natives of St. Raphael, Bellechasse, Quebec. Adelard was born in 1883 and immigrated in 1900. Valerie was born in 1886 and immigrated as a child in 1890. For a number of years, before marrying, both followed the same pattern of working in the winter months in the textile mills of Lawrence, MA, and working on their family farms in Quebec in the summer. Adelard and Valerie married in 1907. They lived in Bradford, near the Wood School. Then, with a growing family, they bought a duplex house on Laurel Avenue, and converted it into a single family home for their 10 children. Valerie died in her 80th year in 1966 and Adelard died 10 years later at the age of 93.

LOUIS AND MAGGIE MELANSON. Louis Melanson was born in Belliveau Cove, Nova Scotia, in 1879. His father, a sea captain, wanted his children to have a safer and better life than he had, so he moved his family to Haverhill when Louis was seven. As with so many others, Louis went to work in the shoe shops as soon as he was old enough to be hired. Marie Margaret "Maggie" Comeau was born in Saulnierville, Nova Scotia, in 1888. She came to Haverhill when she was 17 to live with an aunt and help with the children and the housework. Two years later she married Louis. Their home was at 7 Lafayette Avenue, off Lafayette Square. They had five children.

THE UNION ST. JEAN BAPTISTE. A number of social and fraternal organizations existed for the French Canadians in Haverhill. The most prominent organization was the L'Union de Bienfaisance St. Jean Baptiste, which was founded in 1870. The society's four-story brick quarters in Lafayette Square provided a function hall that was widely used by the Franco community. Space on the street level was rented-out for commercial use, such as the Lafayette Square Pharmacy, owned by Frank Simard.

MEMBERS OF THE ST. JEAN BAPTISTE SOCIETY. The men of the Union are shown in the meeting room of their building in Sargent's, later Lafayette, Square. Some of the men standing in the back row are identified. The first and second from the left are Emil Michaud and Desire Comeau; the fifth from the left is another Comeau; the tall man standing sixth from the left is Louis Thibodeau (known as "Grand Louis" for his height); the third man standing from the right standing is a Rheaume; and at the far right is Ferdinand "Fred" Thibodeau. Among those serving as officers about this time were E. Paquette, A. Chagnon, F.X. Dumont, F. Cloutier, J.B. Laplante, R. Lavalle, and P. Dussault.

THE ORIGINAL ST. JOSEPH'S. The French Canadians who came to Haverhill were predominantly Roman Catholic. When the first families arrived in the 1850s the only church available, St. Gregory's, had an Irish pastor. The Canadians asked for services in their French language. They had their own parish by 1872. It was staffed by French-speaking diocesan priests. A church was completed in 1876 on Grand Street. It was enlarged under Fr. Olivier Boucher in 1888 and space in the basement became classrooms. The Grey Nuns of the Cross from Ottawa staffed the school, and they lived in the basement until an adjacent house on Locust Street was purchased for a convent in 1891.

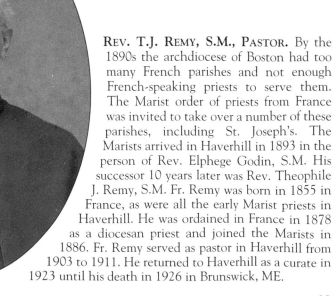

REV. T.J. REMY, S.M., PASTOR. By the 1890s the archdiocese of Boston had too many French parishes and not enough French-speaking priests to serve them. The Marist order of priests from France was invited to take over a number of these parishes, including St. Joseph's. The Marists arrived in Haverhill in 1893 in the person of Rev. Elphege Godin, S.M. His successor 10 years later was Rev. Theophile J. Remy, S.M. Fr. Remy was born in 1855 in France, as were all the early Marist priests in Haverhill. He was ordained in France in 1878 as a diocesan priest and joined the Marists in 1886. Fr. Remy served as pastor in Haverhill from 1903 to 1911. He returned to Haverhill as a curate in 1923 until his death in 1926 in Brunswick, ME.

ST. JOSEPH'S SCHOOL FOR BOYS. The original classroom space for St. Joseph's students had been in the basement of the church on Grand Street. By 1894, space was so limited that the boys were moved to makeshift classrooms in the St. Jean Baptiste Building. A new school was erected at the corner of Broadway and Oak Terrace. The school was staffed, in its early years, by Brothers of the Sacred Heart. According to the Haverhill 1900 City Directory, there were seven brothers teaching 396 boys, or about 56 pupils per class.

FIRST GRADE BOYS. This class of 37 angelic-looking youngsters stands at the front door of St. Joseph's school. The group entered the school in September 1907. By that time, the teaching had been turned over to the Marist brothers, two of whom are shown. Two of the lads in the third row still have their long curls of early childhood, suggesting doting mothers reluctant to part with their "babies!" The Marist brothers staffed the boys' school from 1903 to 1947.

"Thank Heavens for Little Girls!" The girls of St. Joseph's parish would not have their own building until 1912, when a new school was built adjacent to the boys' school. In the interim, the "petites femmes" continued to use the church basement, and possibly some rooms in the convent. The 1900 City Directory gives a 103 Locust Street address and notes that there were 8 "Gray Nuns of Ottawa" to teach 400 girls.

The Girls' Class of 1907. St. Joseph's provided education through grade nine. Some of these young women would go on to St. James High School. A privileged few might be sent by their parents to "convent schools" in Montreal or Quebec. Most went to work. A high school diploma was not yet a necessity. This class consisted of the following, from left to right: (front row) Emma Beauparlant, Antoinette Beaudry, Pauline Chaput, and Corinne Guilmond; (middle row) Beatrice Bourque, Josephine Carrier, Sr. St. Pascal, Corinne Beauregard, Pauline Bourneuf, and Lea Lapierre; (back row) Leontine Prevost, Emma Brouillette, Beatrice Morel, Berthe Daniel, Regina Sinotte, and Alexina Basiliere.

GRADUATES OF THE NEW GIRLS' SCHOOL. A new school for girls opened on February 1913. The upper two floors had classrooms, while the first floor contained not only a large hall for parish functions, but a men's social club room. These 13 young women, the Class of 1913, were the first to graduate from the new building. They are, from left to right, as follows: (front row) Marie Jeanne Gagnon, Laura Dube, Blanche Villeneuve, Marie Louise Brunelle, and Eva Guilmond; (middle row) Yvonne Tremblay, Eugenie Desilet, School Superior Sr. Marie de la Trinite, Sr. Marie-Rachel, Anna Legault, and Blanche Beaulieu; (back row) Lillian Morel, Mathilde Arsenault, Therese Dufour, and Eugenie Sinotte.

FOUR GENERATIONS OF GAUVIN WOMEN. In 1934, 40 years after Lucinda Gauvin posed for the photographer with her husband and children (p. 14), she celebrated the birth of her great-granddaughter. From left to right are Agnes Gauvin Pullen, baby Claire Payette, Bertha Pullen Payette (Claire's mother), and Lucinda Finney Gauvin. They are standing in front of the family home in Lafayette Square.

WILLIAM AND BLANCHE DODIER. Bill Dodier, the 11th child of Louis and Josephine, was born in 1902 in Exeter, NH. His parents came from Trois Rivieres, Quebec. In the early 1900s, the Dodiers moved to Haverhill and Louis bought a large tract of land on which he built his house. As each child grew to adulthood and married, Louis built a house for him/her. This is the origin of Dodierville on Hilldale Avenue. Bill married Blanche Fournier in 1922. She was born in Gaspe, Quebec, to Francois and Marie Louise Fournier, who later moved to this city. Bill and Blanche were parents to 12 children. These members of the wedding party, from left to right, are as follows: (front row) Blanche and William Dodier; (back row) Adrian Fournier and Alma Dodier.

ALBIN AND MARY DALY GALLANT FROM PEI. The vast majority of French Canadians in Haverhill were from either Quebec or Nova Scotia. Another, smaller number, were Acadians from Prince Edward Island. Albin Gallant came from Miscouche in the French-speaking section of the island. Mary Daly was the descendant of Irish immigrants to the island and her home was in St. Mary's Road in the Montagu area. The common origin overcame ethnic differences and the two were married c. 1913. Albin and Mary Gallant set up housekeeping in Bradford. Albin was in the ice business. The couple is shown with their son John and daughter Cecilia. Two other children, Maurice and Albin, were born later.

GROUNDBREAKING FOR THE NEW CHURCH. On the night of December 17, 1923, St. Joseph's Church and rectory on Grand Street were destroyed by fire. Out of the disaster came an opportunity for a greater consolidation of the parish buildings. The decision was made to rebuild, not on the old site, but in the middle of the French neighborhood on Broadway. The pastor, Fr. Hernin Perennes, had been at St. Joseph's since 1917 as both curate and pastor. He is shown with shovel at the groundbreaking in early 1924. Beside him is the Marist Provincial, Rev. Henri de LaChappelle, a native of France and a member of the French aristocracy. In the Marist tradition of rotating positions, Fr. de LaChappelle went from Provincial to curate in 1924.

THE NEW ST. JOSEPH'S. The magnificent new church that rose majestically atop Pecker's Hill was made of Pennsylvania brick with yellow limestone trim. Ironically, the business of brickmaking, which first employed many of the first Canadian immigrants, no longer existed in Haverhill. The grand church could hold 1,400 worshippers. Its cornerstone was laid in November 1924 and the first Mass was said at midnight on Christmas Day, 1925. A new rectory and convent were also built at this time. This scene is of the dedication of the new buildings later the next year.

Two

THE ITALIANS

THE BOCCIA COURT ON RIVER STREET. Immigrants from Italy began to appear in Haverhill in the 1870s. They settled to the west of the Boston & Maine Railroad station on Washington Street and alongside the Merrimack River on a muddy path that would become River Street. The first Italian families came from the north of Italy, around the Genoa area. They brought with them not only their language and customs, but also their entertainments, such as bocce. These men were at the boccia court built at the rear of 56 River Street. Shown here are, from left to right, Joseph Fopiano (born 1851, immigrated 1872), a fruit dealer; Victor Gardella (born 1861, immigrated 1875) a grocer; Angelo Gardella, a carpenter; Augustino Cosio (born 1882, immigrated 1900), a laborer; and Antonio Stefano Gardella, a grocer and pioneer Italian immigrant.

ANTONIO STEFANO GARDELLA. "Stephen" Gardella was born in Neirone, Genoa, Italy, in 1844, the second of six children. As a young man in his 20s, he fought with the army of General Garibaldi for the unification of Italy. He kept his red soldier's shirt and campaign medals until he died, and wore them at each special event of the Garibaldi Club, which he helped to found. Stephen married Luigina Innocenza in 1870, and with his younger brother, Francesco, moved to Haverhill in 1873. Stephen and Louise had two children, Joseph and Mary. Stephen died at the age of 93 in 1937; Louise died at the same age in 1943.

FRANCESCO GARDELLA AND FAMILY. Francesco was the fifth child of Josephus and Maria Gardella, and was born in Neirone in 1851. Soon after he and his brother Stefano arrived in Haverhill, he married Maria Celestina Garaventa in Boston. They had four sons and two daughters. Both girls and one boy died young. The Gardella brothers had a retail fruit business on Merrimack Street until high rent pushed them to other sections of town. Francesco and his sons set up a fruit business on Main Street and Stefano opened a grocery and bakery on River Street. Shown here, from left to right, are as follows: (front row) Joseph (1888–1953), Celestina (1854–1890), John (1881–1972), Francesco (1851–1937), and Michael (1883–1960); (back row) Maria Rosa (1878–1896).

30

THE GARDELLA BROTHERS FRUIT
STORE. The Gardella brothers arrived
in Haverhill on October 15, 1873.
Before the year ended they had rented
a piece of land on Merrimack Street
and built this 10-foot-high store for
their new fruit business. The location
was at the Washington Square end of
the street, an area that still had many
frame houses on it. They were in
business at that site for 18 years until
the surging transformation of
downtown Haverhill into red brick
shoe shops sent rents skyrocketing.
This photograph was taken in 1883.
Shown here are, from left to right,
Francesco (in the doorway), young
Joseph (1872–1935, standing), and his
father, Stefano.

THE GARDELLA BOARDINGHOUSE.
Between 1873 and 1890, when this
photograph was taken, the
Gardella brothers were joined in
their River Street neighborhood by
dozens of other Italian immigrants.
Multi-family housing was quickly
constructed, including this three-
story house put up by the brothers.
Located at 56 River Street, it
served as a boardinghouse for
family members and for fellow
Genoese.

31

JOSEPHUS ANTONIUS GARDELLA.
Josephus, or Guiseppe, was the patriarch of the Gardella family. He was born December 8, 1813, in Italy and died in Haverhill on October 25, 1902. His longevity was a trait that his children inherited. Among his Haverhill children was Rose (1854–1933), who married Peter Botto. His third son, Giovanni, took up residence at the other end of the country, in Pasadena, CA.

LORENZO AND MARIA LUDAVICA GARDELLA. "Mary Louise" Gardella (1849–1946) was born in Neirone, Genoa. When she was five her mother died. Her father, Josephus, re-married two years later and took the younger members of his family to New York City. They did not return to Italy until 1864. Mary Louise was back in New York in 1866. She married "Lawrence" Gardella (1851–1919) and with two young children they moved to Haverhill to join her brothers. Lawrence and Mary had 11 children. The family lived on Ayer Street. Lawrence ran a grocery store with Amelio Senno at 58 River Street, next to the Gardella boardinghouse. Like many immigrants with rural roots, they also rented land "out in the country" to farm in their spare time.

MICHAEL CASAZZA. Michael (1852–1920) was the husband of the youngest of the Gardella siblings, Maria Magdalena (1859–1935). They married in 1877. Like his in-laws, Michael had a fruit store. It was located at 159 Washington Street, and his family lived above the store. Shown with Michael in this 1905 photograph is his daughter Theresa (1889–1929). She married Mark Calvi and died in childbirth in 1929. Visible to the right of Michael in this picture is the bakery of James Jordan, an Irish immigrant.

FRED AND MARY CHIAPPE. Mary Gardella, the only daughter of Stefano and Louise, was born in New York in 1873. She married Fred Chiappe in 1891, the year he immigrated. Fred was a "lunchpeddler." They lived at 131 River Street. The Chiappes had no children. Fred died in 1912, at age 42, and Mary married William Smyrniotes. She died in 1959.

THE FIRST ITALIAN BAR IN HAVERHILL. There is a common pattern for most immigrant groups and Haverhill is no exception. The immigrant who wishes to be economically independent usually provides a service that his fellow countrymen want and need —hence, the great popularity of grocery stores. But man does not live by food alone—thus the popularity of drinking establishments. This first Italian-owned bar was on River Street. Behind the counter are, from left to right, Lorenzo Gardella (p. 32), Philip Araldo (p. 41), and Joseph Martini (1860–1927), who married Teresa Carbone (p. 37).

THE BOWLEY SCHOOL. The rapid influx of Italian, as well as Jewish, Polish, Armenian, and Lithuanian, immigrants to the western end of Haverhill put great pressure on the city's school system. A number of new schools were built including the Bowley School, built in 1883 on Washington Street and named for land developer Edwin Bowley. Three of Francesco Gardella's children are in this picture. In the dark dress is Maria Rosa (front left); in front of the open space is Michael (third boy in the second row); and in the light-colored shirt is John Gardella (in the back row, second from the left). The Bowley School burned in 1907 and was not rebuilt, but was replaced by the much larger Moody School on Margin Street.

THE GARDELLA BROTHERS MAIN STREET STORE. Francesco Gardella opened his own fruit business at 6 Main Street in the early 1890s. In time he was joined by all three of his surviving sons. Eventually he retired from daily work, but his sons continued the store. Shown in the interior of the store are, from left to right, John Gardella, Louis Chiesa (who had his own fruit store at 42 Main Street), Joseph Gardella, and Michael Gardella.

MILLVALE DAM CONSTRUCTION. Not all Italians who came to Haverhill became permanent residents. One group of families spent a season living in tents in the city. They were the workers, with their wives and children, who had been hired to dig out a reservoir and construct a dam on Millvale Creek to provide an additional water source for the growing population of Haverhill. Their padrone, or boss, was Donato Cuozzo, whose construction company was located in Brooklyn, NY. The workers went from job to job for Cuozzo, living "in the rough" at their construction sites.

THE CHICK BROS. SHOE FACTORY. When the Chick brothers moved to Haverhill to make their fortune in the booming shoe industry, they chose the very outskirts of the built up section of town, out by the old circus grounds on River Street. Their factory, and the others that soon sprang up in that neighborhood, served as a magnet for new streets, new housing, and new immigrants. The facial features of the men in this 1899 photograph suggest they might be some of the many Italian, Jewish, and Armenian immigrants who had recently arrived in the area.

AGOSTINO FORTE AND DAUGHTERS. Agostino (center) worked in the Chick Factory and lived nearby at 51 Maxwell Street. He was born about 1872 in Bisegna, Abruzzi, east of Rome. He immigrated in 1902 as did his wife, Liberato. He is shown here with his friend, Mr. Mugavero, and Forte's four daughters—Susie (born 1911), Nettie (born 1906), Minnie (born 1903), and Carmen (standing, born 1907).

36

CECILIA AND GIOVANNI BUONO CARBONE. Cecilia Vicini (*c.* 1840–1918) and Giovanni Buono Carbone (1829–1893) were married in Recco, south of Genoa on Italy's Riviera. Giovanni was a custom shoemaker and Cecilia ran a store. They had 17 children, all of whom survived to adulthood. On the advice of their father, who was wary of the turmoil in newly unified Italy, the two oldest sons, Angelo and Luigi (Louis), immigrated to Haverhill. They were followed in a few years by their parents and 12 of their 15 siblings. Two sisters stayed at home, and a fisherman brother drowned off Recco Harbor.

CECILIA CARBONE AND CHILDREN. By the time that Cecilia and her children gathered for this family portrait, her husband and sons, Angelo and Michele, had died. Shortly after the picture was taken, Alessandro and Cesare (Charles) returned with their families to Italy. They are, from left to right, as follows: (front row) Teresa Martini (1866–1953), Louis (1859–1945), Cecilia, August (1874–1964), and Matilda Araldo (1868–1939); (middle row) James (1872–1945), Fizia Oneto (1880–1950), Federico (1884–1924), Rosa Assunta Monte (1863–1940), and Victor (1871–1942); (back row) Alex (1877–1954), John (1882–1983), and Charles (1878–c. 1955).

THE CARBONE BROS. STORE. The Carbone brothers had both a wholesale and a retail fruit business. The wholesale business was on Washington Street near the Boston & Maine Railroad Depot. The retail business was in Washington Square, where these three brothers are in this 1888 picture. From left to right are Michael (1862–1902), Angelo (1857–1892), and "Gustie," or August.

THE WASHINGTON STREET STORE, 1892. John and August stand in front of the family store in Railroad Square. The decorations commemorate the 400th anniversary of Columbus' voyage. The Carbone delivery wagon in front is similarly decorated. The driver is James Berisso, whose sister Josephine married James Carbone. This space is now a park that honors Columbus.

LOUIS AND MARIA CHIAPPI CARBONE. Maria Chiappi married Angelo, the oldest Carbone child. Angelo died in January 1893, a few months after his son Louis was born. A few weeks later Angelo's father died. Maria decided to take her young son back to Italy to raise him. He returned to Haverhill as a teenager, but made frequent extended trips to Recco, Italy, to visit with his mother and family.

THE WATER STREET STORE. Cecilia Carbone, who "controlled the purse" in the family, gave each son a sum of money to buy his own store upon marriage. James had opened a business on Water Street, near White's Corner. When he decided to move to a new location in Walnut Square, he sold his store to his brother August (1874–1964). That is "Gusty" in the center with his eight-year-old son Alfred on the right. The date on the front of the fruit bins commemorates Haverhill's 275th anniversary.

CELESTINA BACIGALOUPO CARBONE. August Carbone returned to Italy about 1900 to serve a term in the army. While visiting relatives near Genoa in 1903 he saw the lovely Celestina Bacigaloupo, who was visiting from Ognio, north of Genoa. She was only 16, but within weeks Gus had married her and returned with her to his mother and family in Haverhill. They were parents to six children. During the 1920s the entire family moved to Italy for a number of years, leaving brother-in-law Filippo Araldo in charge of the store. Celestina died in 1972.

GALLERANI'S STUDIO. A favorite spot for young Italian men to gather was Felice Gallerani's photography studio on River Street. Shown here are, from left to right, as follows: (front row) Joseph Sgro, James Greto, Joseph Medaglia, and Joseph Magliani; (back row) Joseph Davoli. Sgro and Medaglia lived near the studio on River Street. Davoli, Greto, and Magliani lived on Mt. Washington. This photograph was taken *c.* 1911, when Gallerani first opened his studio.

CHRISTOPHER COLUMBUS' ANNIVERSARY. In 1892, the Italian community in Haverhill celebrated the 400th anniversary of Columbus' voyage with a grand parade. Riding in this model of the flagship *Santa Maria* are, from left to right, Joseph Gardella, Michael Carbone, a man identified only as "Captain Tonnino," Giovanni Bono Carbone, and Filippo Araldo (Giovanni's son-in-law). Giovanni Carbone, patriarch of the Carbone clan, died the following March at the age of 63.

FILIPPO ARALDO AS CHRISTOPHER COLUMBUS. Araldo had the great honor of portraying the central character in the Columbus commemorative parade. He was born in Italy in 1856, immigrated to Haverhill, and married Matilda Carbone. They had three children. Araldo had a fruit store on Locust Street in the 1890s. During the 1920s, he ran his brother-in-law Gusty's store on Water Street while Gusty's family lived in Italy. He died in 1931.

THE BASSANI FAMILY. Carlo Bassani was born in Italy in 1864 and immigrated in 1889. His wife, Catherine Leone, born in Italy in 1869, immigrated in 1890. Carlo and Catherine married that same year. Bassani was a brick mason and a contractor. Their son John (left), born in December 1890, was killed in action in World War I. The Bassanis lived at various locations in the Lafayette Square area, but moved to Bradford Avenue, Bradford, in 1918.

THE FRANCESCO ONETO FAMILY. "Frank" Oneto was born in Italy in 1866 and immigrated to America in 1883. His wife, Mary, whom he married in 1889, was an 1887 immigrant. They are shown here c. 1895 with daughters Annie (at left, born in 1893) and Carrie (1890–1983), who married John B. Carbone. Frank was listed as a "lunch peddler" in the 1900 census. His lunchroom was at 131 River Street. Frank died about 1913, for that year his wife is listed in the City Directory as a widow.

THE GAIERO FAMILY. Domenic Gaiero (1873–1964) and Mary Rubino (1883–1962), were married in 1902 in their home area of Cuneo, Italy. They were in Haverhill the next year, when their first child was born. This photograph was taken about 1914, the year baby Romeo was born. The Gaieros broke with the usual pattern of Italian immigrants by establishing a home at 470 Primrose Street. They had a fruit store on Locust Street. Shown here are, from left to right, as follows: (front row) Domenic (with Richard), Frank, and Mary (with Romeo); (back row) Louis and Theodore. Three more children were born after this picture was taken.

THE CHARLES GARDELLA FAMILY. Charles (1863–1945) and Franchesca (1875–1964) were married in Genoa, Italy, in 1892. They immigrated to Haverhill in 1896 after their daughter Jennie was born. Seven more children were born in Haverhill. All four of the children's grandparents were named Gardella, indicating how common that surname was in the Genoa area. Charles was a shoe worker and the family lived on Maxwell Street. Pictured are, from left to right, as follows: (front row) Charles, Franchesca, and Victor; (back row) Angelo, Eva, Jennie, Katherine, and Anthony. Nine years after Victor was born, the family had two more daughters, Frances and Romilda.

PASQUALINA DEFAZIO AND CHILDREN. Pasqualina Rizzo and Annibale DeFazio, both born in 1882 in Nicastro, Calabria, were married in 1900. Annibale came alone to Haverhill to earn enough money to bring over his family. He made a number of trips back home. Finally, in 1913, Pasqualina and the children arrived at Ellis Island. This photograph was taken soon afterwards. From left to right are Pasqualina, Joseph (who died in 1919), Mary, and Rose. The DeFazios had nine children altogether, and they ran a market at 491 Hilldale Avenue for 40 years. In later years, their son Ernie took over the running of the store. Annibale died in 1958 and Pasqualina in 1964. They celebrated their 50th wedding anniversary in 1950.

SCHIAVONI'S BARBER SHOP. Giacomo "James" Schiavoni had a bootblack and barber shop in the Coombs building at the corner of Emerson Street and Washington Square. James (1874–1935), his wife, Antoinette (1880–1967), and their family lived on West Street.

BISEGNA FIRST REUNION. Bisegna is east of Rome in the province of Abruzzi. Many Haverhill Italians who immigrated around the turn of the 20th century came from that area, including the Fortes, Bolognas, Contes, and DiPietros. This is one part of a large photograph of the crowd at the first annual outing for people from Bisegna.

THE IUELE FAMILY. The first Italian families in Haverhill had come from northern Italy, particularly from the area around Genoa. This was the prosperous, industrialized section of Italy. After 1900, the immigrants came increasingly from the central and southern areas of the country. This was farming territory where years of poor soil and bad crops had caused widespread poverty. James and Mary Iuele were part of of large group of families who had come from San Pietro, Amaida, in the province of Catanzaro. Shown here, from left to right, are as follows: (front row) Anthony, Mary, Josephine, and Frank Iuele; (back row) James (1878–1949) and Mary Iuele (1888–1988) and cousin Nicola Selvaggio (1891–1976).

THE PALLARIA WEDDING. Domenic Pallaria and Mary Giampa, who married in August 1923, were both born in San Pietro, Amaida. Domenic, born in 1895, immigrated when he was 18. He had been an apprentice blacksmith in Italy, and continued the trade with his father in Haverhill. Mary, the daughter of Giuseppe and Mariarosa Giampa, came as an infant in 1905. The wedding party included the following, from left to right: (front row) Betty Palleria, Mary Giampa, Gilda Davoli, Domenic Pallaria, and Nello Pacci; (back row) Elizabeth "Petina" Serratore and Antonio Selvaggio. Domenic died in 1975; Mary died 20 years later.

THE SCAMPORINO FAMILY. Vincenzo (1863–1941) and Lucia Misenti Scamporino (1866–1940) were married in Syracusa, Sicily, in the mid-1880s. When their first two sons, Emilio and Pietrino, left for America in 1902, there were already eight children in the family. In 1909, Vincenzo came to America to join his sons and prepare for the rest of his family to join them. There were then 12 children in the family. Lucia and eight of the children immigrated in 1911 but two others, Settimo and Virginia, were ill when they arrived and were sent back to Italy to live with relatives for the next two years. In the interim, Raymond, the 13th child, was born. Vincenzo had a little store at the corner of River and Ayer Streets where he made and sold a kind of sherbert, "zelinto." Many of his children and grandchildren were connected with the restaurant business including the Victory Diner, the Lido Cafe, the original Roma Restaurant, DiBurro's, and Ralph's Restaurant in Haverhill. Shown here, from left to right, are as follows: (front) Raymond; (first row) Romeo, Pietrino/Peter, Vincenzo, Lucia, Emilio, and Elena/Helen; (second row) Ottavio/John, Geoffredo, Virginia, Guido, and Aldina/Alice; (third row) Egida/Patsy, Amilcare/George, and Settimo.

THE ITALIAN BAND. The first Italian band in Haverhill poses with friends and family in 1911. The men are listed with their instruments, in order to help identify them. From left to right, they are as follows: (sitting) Pietro Falluchi and Michele Lupi (valve trombones), Giovanni Forte (snare drum), Nando Comforti (bass drum), Enrico Spera (clarinet), and Dominic Pecce and Oliveri Carozza (trumpets); (kneeling at left) Frank Emilio (snare drum) and Ferdinando Scatamacchia (cymbals); (standing) Giuseppe Spera (valve trombone), Pietro Comforti (baritone), Pietro Calvani (flute), Antonio DiPirro (trumpet), and Band Leader Pietro Yannelli (standing in the center wearing a white vest).

THE WITHERELL & DOBBINS BUILDING. A major change to the landscape in the Italian neighborhood west of the railroad tracks took place in 1907. A new raised railroad bridge, to eliminate a grade crossing, and a new passenger bridge across the Merrimack, the County Bridge, helped develop the western end of the city. The Witherell & Dobbins Building, now known as The Viewpoint condominiums, was built where River and Washington Streets met the County Bridge. The contractors employed many Italian brick masons and carpenters in its construction, including Frank Oberti (fifth from the left, second row from the top, in the dark shirt).

THE OBERTI FAMILY AT THE BEACH. Antonio Oberti (1854–1932) and his wife, Louisa Baciagalupo (1867–1926), both immigrated from Genoa, Italy, in 1872. Their sons, Frank and Ralph, had moved to Bradford by 1913, and Antonio and Louisa moved there by 1916. The family is shown vacationing at Plum Island c. 1910. they are, from left to right, as follows: (first row) Louis (1900–1913) and Ida Oberti (1897–1967); (second row) Margherita Gastaldi, the family dog, and Amelia Gastaldi Mortola; (third row) Louisa and Antonio Oberti; (fourth row) Frank and Ralph Oberti and John Medaglia, who married Annie Oberti.

WILL YOU REWARD FAITHFUL, CONSCIENTIOUS SERVICE WITH A SECOND TERM?

FRANK A. OBERTI
Candidate for Republican Nomination as Representative
SECOND TERM

STATE PRIMARIES, SEPTEMBER 23

Wards 5 and 7, Haverhill, Georgetown, Boxford, Groveland

THE RECORD PRESS, HAVERHILL, MASS.

AN OBERTI CAMPAIGN POSTER. Frank A. Oberti, the son of immigrants Antonio and Louisa, became the first person of Italian ancestry to represent Haverhill at the State House in Boston. He served two terms as a representative after World War I. After his terms ended, he returned to the house construction business with his brother Ralph, specializing in a particularly popular "bungalow" style, many samples of which can still be found throughout the city.

MARGHERITA GASTALDI. Margherita Gastaldi (1889–1983), who immigrated in 1900, married Frank A. Oberti (1885–1944) in 1919. They had one son, Frank A. Oberti II. The elder Frank went to work at the Charlestown Navy Yard during World War II, and he died there in a tragic accident. This photograph of Margherita dates from *c.* 1910, when such large hats were in vogue.

THE GUAETTA WEDDING. Antonio Guaetta was born in Sicily in 1895. Soon after he arrived in America, he joined the army and served in World War I. After the war, he moved to Haverhill. He married Angelina Bitonti (1896–1984), a native of Calabria, on May 23, 1920. Guaetta was a barber and maintained a shop at 21 Main Street until 1970. The Guaettas lived in Bradford and had two daughters, Domenica and Mary (who married Frank Oberti II). Antonio died at the age of 104 in 1999.

ANTHONY AND CONZOLATA SCHIAVONI. Anthony Schiavoni (1874–1951) and Conzolata Fabiano (1882–1962) were both from Sansossio, Avellino, Italy. They married in March 1907 and, soon after, immigrated to Haverhill. They lived among the Irish and the Greeks in the "Acre," first on Harrison Street, and then on Driscoll Street. Anthony worked as a laborer for contractors.

THE SCHIAVONI CHILDREN WITH THEIR MOTHER. Conzolata Schiavoni posed about 1919 with six of her children. Two others died, and two, Philip and John, were yet to be born. Shown here are, from left to right, as follows: (front row) Josephine (Mrs. Eugene Yannalfo) and Florence (Mrs. Carl Bavona); (middle row) Pasquale (married Dora Gaudette), Conzolata, and Antoinette (Mrs. Vincent Paolino); (back row) Lena (Mrs. Anthony DeFazio) and Margaret (Mrs. William Ross).

NATALE PARODI. Giovanni Parodi (1856–1943) immigrated in 1879 and was a salesman and fruit dealer. In 1882, he married Giuseppina Oneto (1865–1942), who had immigrated in 1880. They had three children by 1900. Natale, their only son, was born in 1887 and was the first graduate of Haverhill High School from an Italian family. He was awarded a Medal for Heroism for saving a life in 1903. Parodi worked as a clerk in his father's store and eventually became a city police officer.

EMMA PARODI. Emma was the daughter of Giovanni and Josephine Parodi. She was born in 1898, graduated from Haverhill High School, and was the first Italian-American public school teacher. She taught at the Portland Street School in the 1920s and lived with her parents in the "Highlands" at 39 Sheridan Street. Natale and Emma also had a sister, Emanuela (1892–1965).

Three
THE ARMENIANS

EARLY ARMENIAN IMMIGRANTS. The Armenian people, living in the old Ottoman Empire, underwent a horrible massacre in the 1890s. Many of the survivors began a long exodus, which, for some, ended in Haverhill. As with the other immigrants to Haverhill at that time, the local shoe shops were the lure, especially the newer shops on River Street. Five of these men were Antaramian brothers from Khoolu. They were shoe workers. The photograph was taken about 1894. From left to right are Hagop, Antaram, Garabed, Abraham, and Sarkis Antaramian. The man at the far right remains unidentified.

THE KOCHAKIANS. Stephen Kochakian (1869–1933) was the first of his family to come to America. Orphaned by the Turks, he had been raised by his aunt Vartouhee. He immigrated to Nashua, NH, in the mid-1890s. With money he sent home, his aunt improved the family farm, then sent her older son, Garabed, to America. Stephen and Garabed joined the Klondike Gold Rush for a while before returning to Stephen's farm in Hudson, NH. Donabed arrived in 1900 and the three men, with their wives, eventually moved to Haverhill. From left to right are brothers Garabed (1877–1908) and Donabed, their cousin Stephen, and Stephen's wife, Badaskhan (1869–1939).

THE KOCHAKIAN FAMILY IN THE OLD COUNTRY. The Kochakians brothers were from the Harpoot area of Turkey. In the center of this photograph is their mother, Vartouhee Danielian Kochakian, who came to America. Their older sister, her husband and child (left), and their younger sister (right) are assumed to have been killed in the 1915 massacre, as they were never heard from again. Cousin Housep Koochakian (standing in the rear) was educated at Euphrates College, Harpoot. He taught leather cutting in Haverhill and then moved to Brooklyn, NY.

THE GULEZIAN FAMILY IN THE OTTOMAN EMPIRE. The Gulezian family came from Arabkir, Armenia, in eastern Turkey. The father, Hovannes, and the eldest son, Assadour, were killed in the 1895 massacre. The rest of the family came to America. From left to right are as follows: (front row, seated) grandson Bedros/Peter (1890–1970), son of Assadour and Zermita; (middle row) Sarkis, mother Mariam Tavitian Gulezian (1842–1937); Mardiros; and Garabed (1881–1943); (back row) Zermita (1874–1938), widow of Assadour; Hovsanna Gulezian; Perlantoo Chakmar (1878–1967), the wife of Kirkor Gulezian; Makroohy (1883–1961), the wife of Mardiros; and Lucia (1890–1912), the wife of Garabed. Sons Mugurdich and Kirkor (1867–1953), who aren't shown here, were the first to immigrate. They came to Newburyport, then sent for their mother, wives, sisters (Hovhaness and Bilbil), and brothers, and eventually settled in Plaistow, NH. Over time, the sons moved to Haverhill, one daughter moved to Watertown, and one daughter moved to Lynn.

THE GULEZIANS IN PLAISTOW. A large red brick house in the center of Plaistow, still standing, was the home base for the extended Gulezian family. It was to this house that other Gulezians, and Mariam's Tavitian relatives, came after immigrating and before settling into their own homes. This photograph was taken about 1905 and demonstrates how quickly the Gulezians had become Americanized in their style. From left to right, they are as follows: (front row) Arax; her mother, Nuvart (1884–1915, Mrs. Mugurdich), Makroohy (Mrs. Mardiros); Mariam; Maritza; her mother, Perlantoo (Mrs. Kirkor); Lucia (Mrs. Garabed); and Bilbil Gulezian; (back row) Mugurdich; Mardiros; Bedros/Peter; Kirkor; Garabed; and Sarkis.

MUGURDICH GULEZIAN AND FAMILY. Mugurdich (1872–1944) was one of first of his family to come to the United States. He and his family lived on Blaisdell Street, then on Sheridan Street. Mugurdich was a member of the Armenian Benevolent Union and the Arabkir Union. He was a shoe worker. His first wife, Nuvart, died in 1915. He married as his second wife Satenig Mamigonian (1888–1950). Mugurdich and Nuvart had two daughters. From left to right, they are Arax (1903–1994), who became a lawyer; Mugurdich; Satenig; and Vartuhie (1906–1993), who was an accountant.

56

SARKIS GULEZIAN AND FAMILY,
C. 1924. Sarkis (1884–1965) was the
youngest of the Gulezian sons. He was
just a young boy when his father and
oldest brother were massacred in 1895,
and he was only a few years older than
his nephew Peter. Sarkis and his wife,
Armenoohy (Devejian) (1889–1968),
were married in 1905. The family lived
on High Street in Haverhill and Sarkis
operated a grocery store. By the 1920s he
also had a number of real estate holdings.
From left to right are as follows: (front
row) Aram and Vahey; (back row)
Sarkis, George, and Armenoohy.

MARDIROS GULEZIAN AND FAMILY.
Mardiros (1875–1960) and Makroohy
(1883–1961) immigrated in 1900 and
were married in 1903. Their son, and
only child, Diran, was born in 1908
when the family still lived in Plaistow.
Mardiros, a shoe worker, moved his
family to Ayers Village in 1926. Since
the house was on the trolley line,
relatives visited regularly for "a day in
the country." This photograph was taken
c. 1912, when the family lived on
Shepherd Street, Haverhill.

THE TAVITIAN FAMILY. In addition to her children, Mariam Gulezian also had the company of her Tavitian family, including her sister, Takouhi Chahzbanian, and her brothers, Michael and Boghos. Her brother Boghos came to America with his family in 1913. They lived first at the family home in Plaistow, then moved to Gulezian Place, where Boghos worked in Sarkis Gulezian's store. The Tavitians moved to Bradford where they had their own grocery store. Pictured here are, from left to right, as follows: (front row) Boghos/Paul (1866–1928) and his wife, Doudou (1872–1944); (back row) Mardiros/Martin (born on the Fourth of July, 1904) and Sarkis (born in 1901).

THE TAVITIAN-GULEZIAN PICNIC. This photograph was taken c. 1920. Few of the children have been identified but most of the adults are known. From left to right, the adults are as follows: (front left, seated) Yervant Devejian; (behind Yervant, wearing a suitcoat) Sarkis Tavitian; (front right, seated) Armenhoohy Gulezian and her two daughters, Vartouhie and Arax; (middle row, center) matriarch Mariam Gulezian; Shakar Chekmajian; Perlantoo Gulezian; Maritza Devejian; Maritza Yesaian; and Yeghsa Yesaian; (back row, left) Sarkis Gulezian; Kirkor Gulezian; unknown; Doudou Tavitian; and Boghos Tavitian.

THE ORPHANAGE BOYS. Many Armenian children were left without family during the great massacres of 1895 and 1915. Orphanages were set up all throughout the Mediterranean region. These five boys were from Khoolu and were orphaned in the 1915 massacre. The three standing are Berj Aghkadian, Metzadour Menzigian, and Yezegel Ohanian. They eventually found their way to Haverhill to join former neighbors from the small village of Khoolu.

MRS. BABOYIAN, CENTENARIAN. Mariam Baboyian (1829–1940) lived to her 112th year! She is shown here with her daughter, Haiganoush Danielian (1873–1956), and her son-in-law, Armenag Danielian(1873–1929). Armenag was a nephew of Vartouhee Kochakian. They lived on High Street where Mr. Danielian had a small store.

ARAKEL NALBANDIAN. This scholarly looking man from Harpoot was an educator at Euphrates College, and held a high position in the Armenian Church. He came to America and left his family in Armenia while he tried to earn enough money to bring them over. He lost a leg in an accident. At some point he became acquainted with Donabed Kochakian and Mugurdich Jaffarian and made matches with them and two of his daughters. Nalbandian returned to Armenia and prepared to return to America with his wife, Anna, and their three daughters. Only the eldest daughter, Quher, had gone when he died from complications from his amputated leg.

ANNA ZAKARIAN NALBANDIAN. Anna was the wife of Arakel Nalbandian. After her daughter, Quher, came to America and married Murgurdich Jaffarian, she and her two other daughters joined them. Quher insisted that her younger sisters learn English so she had them attend the Wingate School, though they were both teenagers. Anna was born in 1861 and died in Haverhill in 1906 following an operation.

QUHAR AND MUGERDICH JAFFARIAN. Quhar Nalbandian came to Haverhill by way of Worcester, where she had relatives. She married Mugerdich Jaffarian in November 1900. Quher had been a teacher in Armenia, following in the steps of her father. The Jaffarians set up house on Hillside Street, where their first three children were born. Later, they moved to a three-story house on Bateman Street, off of Hilldale Avenue, which has remained the family home since. Because the house had a large backyard, many wedding receptions for fellow Armenian immigrants were held there.

THE JAFFARIAN FAMILY. Mugerdich and Quher Jaffarian pose about 1918 with the first eight of their ten children. From left to right, they are as follows: (front) Sara; (middle row) Souren, Annie, Quher, Mugerdich, Viola, and Waskin (Walter); (back row) Papkin (Philip), Kurken (who began the family auto business), and Yervant (Edward). Kurken, or Fred as he was better known, was the first child born to Armenian parents in Haverhill.

DANABED AND HAIGOUHEE KOCHAKIAN. Haigougee was the second daughter of Arakel Nalbandian. She married Danabed Kochakian *c.* 1906 and they established a family home on Mt. Dustin Avenue off Hilldale Avenue. Danabed worked in the shoe shops, but he also grew vegetable plants for home gardeners in a greenhouse he attached to his home. This sideline grew into a full-time business. The photograph was taken in the early 1920s. From left to right are as follows: (front row) Rose (1920–) and Vaughan (1917–); (middle row) Haigouhee (1888–1964) and Danabed (1884–1950); (back row) Anna (1910–), Arthur (1907–1988), and Charles (1908–1999).

VARTOUHI DANIELIAN KOCHAKIAN. The Kochakians were part of a large group of Armenian immigrants to Haverhill who came from Khoolu, near Harpoot. Vartouhi (p. 54) was born in 1842. She came to Haverhill to join her son Danabed and her nephews, Stephen Kochakian and Armenag Danielian. This photograph was taken after she suffered a stroke. She died February 1, 1914.

THE KASPARIANS. These three Kasparian men were from the village of Khoolu, as were the Kochakians and the orphanage boys (p. 59). A significant number of Haverhill Armenians came from this small place. Kheyagh (standing, right) is the only one identified by name. The Kasparians lived on High Street.

THE YOUGHIANS. Hovhaness Youghian (1870–1933, seated right), along with his wife, Mary K. (1873–1949), and their son George J. (1907–1986, in his father's lap) were an early family of Armenians in Haverhill. Hovhaness, or John, immigrated in 1895, and his wife in 1901. They lived on Temple Street and had a small store. The others in the photograph are not identified.

YEGAZAR ANTARAMIAN. Yegazar (1882–1967) was the son of Garabed Antaramian (p. 53). He arrived in Haverhill in 1900, leaving his young wife, Mariam Andonian (1885–1952), and month-old daughter, Veron, in Khoolu. His father and most of his uncles had already returned to Turkey. It took Yegazar 12 years to save the money to bring over his family. This picture was taken soon after Mariam's arrival, and she is still in her home attire. The Antaramians are shown with Mariam's uncle, Hovhaness Youghian (seated, left).

THE ANDONIAN FAMILY IN TURKEY. Mariam Andonian Antaramian left her family in Armenia, shown here, to join her husband in Haverhill. Her blond, blue-eyed mother, Joabar, is seated center. Her half-brother, George Aghkadian (standing), fled the 1915 massacre and lived in Marseilles, France. Also standing are her sister, Khartwon Andonian, an unidentified sister, and a child. All but George were killed by the Turks.

THE AMERICANIZED ANTARAMIANS. Only a short while after her arrival in Haverhill, Mariam Antaramian had shed her ethnic dress and taken on the appearance of someone who had been in America for years. Yegazar and Mariam are shown with their daughter Veron and Yegazar's cousin, Baghdazar Antaramian (1888–1973, seated center). Mariam and Veron survived two possible tragedies before arriving in America. They had been in a group rounded up by Turkish soldiers to be massacred when the soldiers were suddenly called to another place. In Liverpool, England, Veron became sick and her mother had to cancel their ship's passage. The ship was the *Titanic*.

THE DEPOIANS. Martin Depoian (1894–1981, right) was a shoe manufacturer in Haverhill by the 1930s. His company was the M. & H. Shoe Co. His father, Harootuin (1857–1941, left), lost his wife, Heghina, in the 1915 massacre. They are shown with their cousin, Marsob Andonian, who was also a cousin of Mariam Antaramian. All three men came from Khoolu.

MOOSHOIAN BROS. BAKERY. Charles and George Mooshoian began a bakery at 200 Essex Street in 1902 and continued in business until 1910. During those years each brother lived in rented rooms in the vicinity of the bakery. By 1910, George had his own home at 26 Primrose Street. A year later, the bakery closed, Charles had returned to Armenia, and George was listed in the City Directory as an "agent" with a home in Bradford. George is the man with the mustache in the doorway of the bakery. Charles is in the delivery wagon. The other men are unidentified.

YERVANT DEVEJIAN. This well-armed warrior is Yervant (Edward) Devejian (1890–1971). He served in the U.S. Army Infantry in World War I, but this uniform more closely resembles that put together by the military company of immigrants sponsored by the Armenian Revolutionary committee. After the war he clerked at the Gulezian store on Washington Avenue and was a butcher at both Ganem's and Handy Dandy Markets on Merrimack Street. Yervant married Maritza Gulezian (1902–1992).

THE ARMENIAN RED CROSS. The women of the Armenian community in Haverhill formed a branch of the Red Cross to aid survivors of the Turkish massacres. This photograph was taken in 1915. Shown here are the following, from left to right: (front row) Mesdames Agnes Ohanessian, Maritza Esperian, Almas Chooljian, Kazanjian, and Mary Kasparian; (back row) Mrs. Michael Tavitian, Mrs. George Mooradian, and Mesdames Haighoohi Katchadoorian, Mariam Antaramian, Haiganoosh Talanian, Haiganoosa Daniclian, and Asterdig Chooljian.

A LIBERTY BOND DRIVE. The Haverhill branch of the Armenian National Union did its part to help the American cause in World War I with a Liberty Bond drive, *c.* 1918. This float was in front of the house of the shoe manufacturing Fox Brothers at 6 Swazey Street. Among those identified are Asterdig Chooljian, Misak Tashjian, Veron Antarmanian, Tateos Tateosian, Dikran Danielian, Maritza Babolian, George Babajian, and Vasjanoush Depoian.

THE ARMENIAN REVOLUTIONARY FOUNDATION. One of the most politically active of the Armenian groups was the Armenian Revolutionary Foundation. They sponsored Armenian volunteers to go to Russia to fight the Turks in World War I, and were also the supporters of the Dashnagzagan Party, which had run the sovereign state of Armenia in the old Russian Empire, before the Bolsheviks took over the empire. The young girl in this 1915 picture is Veron Antaramian; she accompanied her father, Yegazar, to the picnic.

THE ANTARAMIAN FAMILY. Many years removed from Armenia, Yegazar and Mariam Antaramian posed with their children. From left to right are as follows: (front row) Koharig ("Queenie"), Yegazar, Charlie, George, Mariam, and Virginia; (back row) Veron. Soon after this photograph was taken, Veron (1900–1994) married Harry Kazarosian (1898–1977).

THE LEAVITT SHOE COMPANY. Shown in the packing room of the Leavitt Shoe Co. on Duncan Street are, from left to right, Baltazar and Yegazar Antaramian, Bedros Bedrosian, and Harry Kazarosian, son-in-law of Yegazar. At rear center is Kheyagh Kasparian (p. 63). The photograph is dated November 2, 1922. Soon after this, Yegazar was promoted to foreman.

SHOE WORKERS. The common experience to all immigrants to Haverhill in the early 20th century was work in the shoe shops. Danabed Kochakian (left), who began working in the shoe shops soon after his arrival in Haverhill, was still engaged in the same work when this photograph was taken in 1922. The place is probably the Winchell Company on Locust Street. Fourth from the left is Thomas Torosian.

THE MOVSESIAN BROTHERS. The Movsesians were born in Harpoot, Armenia, the sons of Andon and Almas Movsesian. Moses (center), the eldest, was born in 1886 and immigrated to America in 1903. He first went to Fresno, CA, but was in Haverhill by 1904. He was a shoe manufacturer for over 40 years, operating the Modern Shoe Company. Moses died in 1964. Edgar (right) was born in 1896 but didn't move to Haverhill until 1918. He operated the Dainty Maid Shoe Co., and the E and M Fabric Co. Edgar died in 1973. The third brother, Charles (left), lived briefly in Haverhill but took up permanent residence in California.

ARAX GULEZIAN. Arax, the daughter of Mugurdich and Nuvart, was born in 1903. She graduated from Haverhill High School in 1922 and Boston University Law School in 1928. Arax was the first female lawyer in Haverhill's Armenian community. She and her sister Vartuhie moved to Bermuda in the 1950s and lived there for the next 40 years.

SARKIS AND ZARTAR TAVITIAN. Sarkis, the son of Boghos and Doudou (p. 58), was born in Armenia in 1901. The family moved to Haverhill and he graduated from Haverhil High School. In 1927, he and his mother traveled to Marseilles, France, to select a bride from the girls at an Armenian orphanage. Their choice was Zartar/Sarah Hagopian, a lovely 17-year-old girl. They were married on August 13 and returned to Haverhill to set up housekeeping. Sarkis and his brother ran Tavitian's Cash Market on Laurel Avenue in Bradford. He died in 1978. They had three children—Paul, Virginia, and Joseph.

MARTIN AND ESTHER TAVITIAN. Mardiros/Martin Tavitian, born in Armenia on the Fourth of July, 1904, married Esther Vasjabedian in 1934. Esther was born in Baku, Azerbaijan, in the old Russian Empire in 1909. They shared a house and a business with Sarkis. Martin was one of the founders of the famous Fourth of July Wood School playground party and bonfire, which doubled as a birthday party for him. Martin died in 1982 and Esther died in 1990. They had two sons, Michael and Simon.

THE DEEJIAN FAMILY. Sebou Devejian (left) operated a grocery store at the corner of Washington Street and Washington Avenue near the B&M station. He was born in Armenia in 1890 and died in 1969. His wife, Arouseag (1900–1988), is on the right and their son Anthony (born 1928) is in front. Sebou was a brother of Yervant Devejian. The photograph was taken at a picnic in 1932.

THREE MUSICIANS. There are certain traditions that hold an immigrant community together—food, music, and religion are the most familiar. Armenians in Haverhill were not united in religion. Some were Protestant, some Armenian Apostolic, and some Catholic; but all shared a love for their own food and music, which were combined at Armenian picnics. Setrag Simonian (left) plays the "zoorna," or horn, Minas Bozajian (center) poses with his violin, Sarkis Tavitian is strumming the banjo.

Four

THE LITHUANIANS

A Lithuanian Picnic. Lithuanians come from northeastern Europe. Though historically close to the Poles, they are not Slavs, but Balts, and have a language that is unique among European tongues. As with so many of the other groups discussed in this book, they came to Haverhill in the 1890s seeking economic security, but were also fleeing the brutality of the Russian Empire. They settled in Haverhill in the River Street area. This picnic scene dates from about 1910. The violinist on the right is Julius Belsky. The two couples in the center are Peter Yankowsky and Rose Budrick, who married in 1910, and Stanley and Sophie Dzingelevich. The woman on the right is most likely Regina Yankowsky Orlowsky (1880–1912); her husband, Peter Orlowsky (1866–1955), is also shown here. Their 115 River Street home was a boardinghouse for many of their relatives. The three children are Mary, Annie, and Peter Orlowsky.

JULIUS BELSKY AND ANNIE BELSKY STRAVINSKY. Julius was born in Lithuania in 1878 and came to America in 1901. His younger sister Annie was born in 1883 and immigrated in 1904. That same year she married Boltrus Stravinsky (1873–1936), who had immigrated in 1898. Annie and Boltrus and their six daughters lived on River Street. Annie, like Regina Orlowsky, died young—she succumbed to influenza during the epidemic of 1918.

MARTIN AND PETER YANKOWSKY. Martin (left), the younger brother of Peter, was born in Lithuania c. 1892. He immigrated by way of Canada in 1910. His trip to Haverhill was delayed when he ran out of money and could not leave Canada until his brother Peter sent the necessary funds. Like his brother, his first place of residence in Haverhill was with his sister Regina. Martin was a shoe worker. He and his wife, Mary, lived on South Cogswell Street, Bradford. Martin died in the mid-1930s.

PETER YANKOWSKY AND STANLEY DZINGELEVICH. Peter was born in 1886. The family home was near the great city of Vilnius. He immigrated in 1903, and lived with his sister Regina and her husband, Peter Orlowsky, on River Street. He worked in the shoe shops by day and studied the English language in school by night. He was an organizer, and longtime activist, in the Gedemino Club. His friend Stanley is on the right.

ROSE BUDRICK. Rose was born in 1892 in Biozios, Lithuania. She immigrated in 1908 to live with an aunt in North Andover. Rose worked in a textile mill in Lawrence, a short distance away from her aunt's house. She met Peter Yankowsky at a Lithuanian gathering and married him in 1910, at St. James Church.

ROSE BUDRICK WITH SOPHIE AND STANLEY. Sophie (1891–1961, right) and Stanley (1882–1948, center) Dzingelevitch immigrated to Haverhill in 1908. They were best friends with Rose and Peter Yankowsky and married about the same time, in the early 1910s. They lived on Wilson Street and later on Garfield Street. Stan was a laster and Sophie a wood heeler in the shoe shops.

BOATING ON THE LAKE. This picture was probably taken the same day as the picnic in the earlier photograph. It is thought to be at Johnson's Pond, South Groveland, a favorite spot with Peter and Rose Yankowsky, who are at the oars on the nearest boat.

PETER AND ROSE BUDRICK YANKOWSKY.
Peter Yankowsky and Rose Budrick pose
together around the time of their marriage
in 1910. Rose's hat is an eye-catcher! The
couple had two children, Aldona and
Edward. Both Peter and Rose were very
active in the Lithuanian St. George's
Parish. Peter died in 1961 and Rose died in
1983.

THE YANKOWSKY FAMILY. Peter and
Rose pose with their first child, and
only daughter, Aldona, who was born
in 1918. The family lived "on the
hill," as upper Washington Street was
referred to, on Bartlett Street, away
from the River Street/Margin Street
neighborhood, where so many of their
fellow Lithuanians clustered.

THE BELSKY FAMILY. Joanna ("Jennie") Miskinis was born in Lithuania in 1886. She immigrated in 1907, and that same year she married Julius Belsky (p. 74) in Lawrence. The family lived on River Street. Julius was a shoe worker and Jennie a coverer at Brody Wood Heel. Julius was a self-taught violinist much in demand at Lithuanian gatherings. From left to right, they are as follows: (front row) Jennie and sons Joseph and Edward; (back row) Julius and daughter Helen. Julius died in 1952; Jennie died in 1979.

THE ZIMINSKI FAMILY. Alice and Adam Ziminski married in Lithuania in 1892. Adam immigrated in 1905 and Alice followed two years later with their son Joseph and daughter Mary. Two other children died in Lithuania. Two more sons, John and Felix, were born in Haverhill. Adam worked in a hat shop. Just before World War I burst upon Europe, the family, except for Joseph, returned to Lithuania. Son John came back to Haverhill in the 1920s, but the rest of the family stayed in their native place. Pictured here are, from left to right, as follows: (front row) Mary and John Jr.; (middle row) Alice and Adam; (back row) Joseph. Felix was born in 1910, just after this picture was taken.

THE BELRICK FAMILY. Povilas Balevicius (Paul Belrick) was born in Liskiava, Lithuania, in 1876. Anna Ramcykie was born the same year, also in Lithuania. They both immigrated to Lawrence, MA, in 1901 and met each other at work in the mills. Paul and Anna married early in 1903. They had four children in Lawrence and moved to Haverhill c. 1920 where they made their home on Margin Street. Paul worked as a weaver at the Pentucket Mill. Shown here are, from left to right, as follows: (front) Dorothy (born 1911), Paul, and Anthony (born 1916); (back row) Victoria Ramcykie (Anna's sister), Anna, and Natalie/Nellie (born 1909). The oldest son, Frank (born in 1905), had his own home at the time this picture was taken.

THE VENCIUS WEDDING. Michael Vencius (1892–1981) immigrated in 1912 and his wife, Eva M. (1895–1964), immigrated in 1913. They were married about 1917. Their attendants (front) were Peter and Rose Yankowsky. The woman standing on the right was Mary Orlowsky, Peter's niece. Michael was known as a great singer. A shoe worker, he and the rest of the Vencius family made their home first at 364 River Street and then at 91 Wilson Street. For a period of time, Michael was co-owner, with Joseph Jurelionis, of the M & J Cafe on Washington Street.

JOSEPH AND MARY TRUSKA. Joseph and Mary are shown in 1913 at Salisbury Beach. This was about the time they married at St. James Church, Haverhill. Joseph was born in Lithuania in March 1890. He immigrated in 1906 and by 1910 he was boarding with Antoni and Katy Vencis. He was a shoe worker and, for a while, co-owned an undertaking business (Mucciolo and Truska). Mary Cibirka (also known as Smith) was born in 1897 in Haverhill to a Lithuanian father and a Polish mother. They lived on Hilldale Avenue (Collection of Haverhill Historical Society.)

THE TRUSKA FAMILY. Joseph and Mary had one child, Algerd, born in 1915. Mary, a fine singer, was once asked to audition for the Boston Opera Company. She turned down the opportunity but continued to sing for years after the offer. Joseph was an edge trimmer in local shoe shops. He died in July 1953; Mary died in 1987. Her wedding gown was donated to the Haverhill Historical Society. (Collection of Haverhill Historical Society.)

LITHUANIAN PICNIC GROUNDS. In the early 1920s, the Lithuanian community in Haverhill purchased an extensive piece of land off Salem Street in Bradford. One section was set off as a cemetery. The remaining acreage became picnic grounds. This photograph, taken in 1923, is of the original "clubhouse," complete with a dance floor and small stage. A smaller building served as a kitchen. This was a great spot for summertime gatherings and it was widely used by many people, not just Lithuanians. The city of Haverhill bought the picnic grounds for the new Bradford Elementary School.

THE AKSTIN FAMILY. Antanas/Anthony Akstin (1890–1976) immigrated in 1910. His wife, Amelia/Nellie (1894–1967), immigrated in 1913. They were married c. 1917. Tony was a shoe worker. The family lived on View Street, then on Beach Street, before settling down on Buttonwoods Avenue. Shown here are, from left to right, Nellie, their daughter Helen, and Anthony.

THE THREE CHIRUS SISTERS. Jennie and Agatha Chirus, long residents in Haverhill, welcomed their young sister, Malvina, to the city in the 1920s. Jennie was married to Alexander Naudzunas, a shoe worker, and they lived on Margin Street. Agatha was married to Mike Chaikovski. They lived in Haverhill for a while before moving to Portsmouth, NH. Malvina married John Ziminski and they lived on River Street.

FIVE FRIENDS. Mike and Agatha (Chirus) Chaikovski (rear left) join their friends Peter Swain and Victor Slaiciunas (front) and Benigna (Svenciskas) Slaiciunas (rear right). Peter Swain and his wife, Mary, operated grocery stores in Haverhill and Bradford. Victor Slaiciunas was a barber with a home on Groveland Street. All of these people, including Peter's wife, Mary, were post-1910 immigrants from Lithuania.

ANNA DEGASUNAS. Anna was the daughter of Michael and Mary Degasunas. They lived on River Street and Michael was a shoe worker. The family first appeared in the 1921 City Directory, sharing a two-family house with Ralph and Marcella Degasunas. Anna married John Marino *c.* 1932. They lived at 36 Salem Street, Bradford. Her parents, now known as Degasun, moved into 37 Salem Street along with their son Raymond, the proprietor of the Quality Cash Market on River Street.

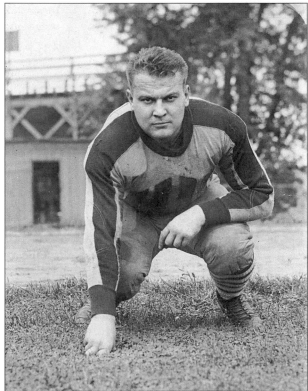

JOE RICH. Joe Rich was an outstanding college football player. He was born in Haverhill in 1912 to Baltrus Richavich (1878–1969) and Elizabeth Zurwell (1889–1961). Baltrus immigrated in 1887 and Elizabeth in 1904. Joe graduated from Haverhill High School and was a star member of the football team. After attending Dean Academy, he went to Columbia University and was on the football team that went to the 1934 Rose Bowl, where they upset Stanford 7-0. Joe was a classic 60-minute, all-around player. After college, he was a salesman and lived in New York City.

MARCELLA NARKUN TAKES A RIDE. Marcella (left) was born in Lithuania in 1880. She immigrated to America in 1899 and soon after married Joseph Narkun (1870–1941). They had four children—Frank, Anna, Pauline, and William. Joe was a shoe worker and Annie was a weaver in the textile mill. She supplemented her income during Prohibition with a popular "home brew" that her children remembered delivering in a straw suitcase, via the trolley cars, to customers in Salem, NH. Marcella put her profits into real estate by purchasing three triple-decker houses on Washington Avenue. Neither the other couple, nor the horse, have been identified. Marcella died in 1966.

ANNA NARKUN. Anna, born in 1905, was the second child and first daughter of Marcella and Joe Narkun. The 1930 City Directory listed Annie as rooming in her parents' home on Central Street but being employed in New York City. In this photograph, she strikes a sporting pose in her 1920s knickers, a 100% American "flapper."

PETER PAICIUS/POTH. Peter was born in Brooklyn, NY, to immigrant parents in 1906. He moved to Haverhill in his late teens, the only one of his family to do so. Peter worked in shoe shops, including Allen Shoe, and was an active member of Gedemino Club.

PETER AND ANNA (NARKUN) POTH. Perhaps there was a connection between Peter's coming from Brooklyn, NY, and Anna's working in New York City for a while. Whatever the reason, Peter and Anna found each other and married in the early 1930s. They had two children, Barbara and Matthew. The family lived on Ashworth Terrace. Anna died in 1980 in her 75th year. Peter died in 1992, aged 86.

JOSEPH ZIMINSKI AND FAMILY. Joseph was born in Lithuania in 1895 and came to Haverhill in 1907. When his parents decided to return to their home, Joe chose to stay in Haverhill. He and Margaret (1896–1972) were married c. 1922. Joe was a stock fitter. The family lived on Eudora Street. Joe died in 1956. Pictured are, from left to right, Margaret, their daughter Alice, and Joseph.

THE ZIMINSKI WEDDING. John Ziminski was born in Haverhill in 1907 but went to Lithuania with his parents c. 1913. After World War I and the collapse of the Russian Empire, John left the newly independent Lithuanian Republic to return to Haverhill. He boarded with his brother Joseph until marrying Malvina Chirus. The Ziminskis operated John's Market on River Street for many years. Shown in this 1934 wedding picture are, from left to right, unknown, Anna Pilsucki (1890–1953), John Austin (Aukstanas), Alice Chaikovski (Malvina's niece), John Ziminski (1907–1990), and Malvina Chirus (1905–1986).

THE GEDEMINO CLUB. The Lithuanian men organized the Gedemino Club in 1910 for the purpose of "establishing and maintaining a place for a reading room and social meetings." Their clubhouse on the corner of River and Margin streets was completed by 1914. Many of the original members were still alive when this 1935 photograph was taken. Only the men in the first, second, and fourth rows can be identified, suggesting that the others were visitors. They are, from left to right, as follows: (first row) J. Kazukonis, unidentified, S. Zaremba, unidentified, Verbickas, unidentified, unidentified, Bakanosky, Klimauskas (1), Klimauskas (2), A. Kazukonis, unidentified, Wm. Kazukonis, and J. Kaminski; (second row) unidentified, unidentified, Aidukonis, unidentified, W. Chaplick, Chernesky, J. Becksha, Stan Dzingelevitch, Anthony Akstin, J. Akstin, ? Akstin, Dr. J. Grevis, W. Putis Sr., S. Benkus, and Paul Belrick; (third row) A. Mayauskas, all others unidentified; (fourth row): all unidentified; (fifth row) unidentified, J. Buya, D. Benkus, E. Mikonis, Zaremba, A. Kazlauskas, M. Benkus, D. Uzdavinis, P. Palauskas, A. Navickas, unidentified, S. Uzdavinis, unidentified, J. Ziminski, M. Vencis, J. Kuliesh, Abromovitch, M. Matonis, and unidentified.

THE RUTKAUSKAS FAMILY. John and Rose Rutkauskas were well-known as merchants and for their political connections. John (1885–1967) immigrated in 1902. Rose Andrusciewicz (1892–1967) immigrated in 1910. For many years they operated a dry goods store at 171 Washington Street. They had two children—John (1916–1999) became an engineer and Anna (1914–1996) married James P. "Jake" Rurak, who served as a state senator in Massachusetts from 1959 to 1976. The Rutkauskas' grandson, James A. Rurak, became mayor of Haverhill. Shown here are, from left to right, John and Constance Rutkauskas, John and Rose Rutkauskas, and Anna and James P. "Jake" Rurak.

PETER YOCUMSKI. Peter was a later generation of Lithuanian. He operated Peter's Restaurant, a popular luncheonette near the Bixby building and the B&M Railroad overpass on Washington Street. He and his wife, Mary, lived at 115 River Street.

THE INTERIOR OF ST. GEORGE'S CHURCH. Lithuanians first acted to have their own church in 1911. They bought land on River Street near the baseball grounds. They already had the designation of a parish dedicated to St. George, patron of Lithuanians. They ended up purchasing the Mt. Washington Universalist Church on Washington Street at Gilbert Avenue. It had been built in 1892. This is a photograph of the interior, decorated for Eucharistic Adoration on Holy Thursday. The altar boys are Edmund Yankowsky (left) and Edward Amshey (right), who died in 1999.

A LITHUANIAN INDEPENDENCE DAY CELEBRATION. One of the most important days each year for American Lithuanians is February 22, when Lithuania's independence from Russia is commemorated. In Haverhill, the day was always marked by a program of speeches and entertainment at Gedemino Hall. This photograph is from the 1953 celebration. Shown here are, from left to right, as follows: (front row) Rev. Gerald Matejune, C.P.; Peter Yankowsky; and Rev. Vaclavas Paulauskas; (back row) Marcella Matonis; Prof. Alphonse Lesinskas of Merrimack College; Anthony Radzukinas; Ben Jurkevicius; Peter Svirskas; and Sophie Verbickas.

LADIES' SODALITY, 50TH ANNIVERSARY. The oldest women's organization for Lithuanians was a religious group, Our Lady's Sodality, begun in 1910. Members are, from left to right, as follows: (front row) Josephine Larkin, Rose Yankowsky, Anna Cardran, Sophie Dzingelevitch, Pauline Wersoski, Marcella Matonis, and Sophie Verbickas; (back row) Mary Zakarosky, unidentified, unidentified, Anna Radzukinas, and Anna Walukevich.

GEDEMINO CLUB OFFICERS. The Gedemino Club carried the name of Gedyminas, a heroic medieval Lithuanian knight-warrior. The installation of new officers for the Gedemino Club in 1951 included many men whose roots could be traced back to the first Lithuanian immigrants in Haverhill. The officers are, from left to right, as follows: (front row) Jacob Vitkauskas, Paul Welsch, Joseph Walch, Joseph Belsky, and Atty. William Kiarsis; (back row) Paul Macksvitis, Peter Yankowsky, John Kancevitch, John Kuliesh, and Stanley Kuliesh.

Five

THE POLES

THE DEDICATION OF ST. MICHAEL'S CHURCH. The first Poles arrived in Haverhill in the mid-1890s. They were only a few to begin with, but by January 1901 their numbers had so increased that they began to plan for their own church. In 1909, a parcel of land was acquired at the corner of High and Swasey Streets, and a pastor, Rev. Dr. Alexander Syski, was appointed. The first Mass in the new church was said on January 1, 1911, and the building was officially dedicated on September 17, 1911. In this photograph, the clergy who had gathered at the Temple Street residence of Fr. Syski prepared to process to the new church. Bishop Joseph Anderson, auxiliary bishop of Boston (seated), presided at the ceremonies. Seated next to the bishop is Fr. James O'Doherty, pastor of St. James Church, and the dean of Haverhill priests. Fr. Syski is behind the bishop. The lovely little girls (front) are in traditional Polish dress.

ST. MICHAEL'S POLISH CATHOLIC CHURCH. St. Michael's Church was built in 1910 and dedicated in 1911. The contractor was John Martin Roche, who had just completed the new Haverhill High School on Summer Street. The architect, Harrison Atwood of Dorchester, had designed the Mission-style building, with the exterior shape influenced by the Franciscan Mission churches of California. The original windows were of plain tinted, leaded glass.

ST. MICHAEL'S INTERIOR. The original interior decor of the church was intended to remind viewers of the national colors of Poland. The floor was of a dark apple green with a lighter shade of green on the side walls rising to a sky blue ceiling. The windows were of tinted green glass and the great oval window in the choir loft was of green with a blue cross. The vaulted ceiling required no obstructing pillars. The original pulpit was 10 feet high with a metal hood. St. Michael's survived as a parish until the summer of 1998, when it was combined with Haverhill's other ethnic parishes—St. Joseph's for the French, St. Rita's for the Italians, and St. George's for the Lithuanians—into one territorial parish named, appropriately, All Saints.

THE HOLY ROSARY SOCIETY. This was the oldest church society in the parish. It was formed in March 1911 for the women to "preserve the faith and traditions of their people from the fatherland." Charter members were Mesdames Mary Orlowski, Julia Kowalewski, Magdalena Anuszewski, Sophie Lesiczka, Mary Masloski, Helen Dempski, and Mary Zawacki. Other members included Misses Agnes Lesiczka, Sophie Wos, Mary Kalinowski, Katherine Kopec, Anna Bielicka, Frances Bielicka, Katherine Delekta, Mary Delekta, Sophie Delekta, Anna Szeliga, and Josephine Pierog.

WALENTY AND SOFIA LESICZKA. Walenty Lesiczka (1880–1936) and Sofia Szeliga (1890–1965) immigrated from Poland in 1906 and were married about 1910. They were two of the founders of the Polish Saint Michael's Parish in Haverhill. Walenty is in the uniform of the Saint Michael the Archangel Society. The society began in 1901 and was the first Polish organization in Haverhill. Sofia is in traditional Polish dress.

JULIA KOSCIOLAK KOWALESKI. Julia Kosciolak, and her sister Caroline (right) were born in Ulanow, in the Austrian part of divided Poland. Julia (1879–1956) immigrated in 1895. In 1899, she married Julius Kowaleski (1872–1926). He had immigrated in 1892 from his home in Bialystock in the Russian part of Poland. Julia's sister Caroline immigrated later and stayed with Julia until marrying Joseph Sucholdoski. Caroline and Joseph eventually moved to Lawrence with their five children.

A PARISH PICNIC. The youthfulness of the Polish immigrants to Haverhill is evident in this picture. In general, few multi-generational families immigrated. Rather, young men and women came alone or with siblings or cousins. Marriage matches were made on this side of the ocean. Two events help to date this picture to c. May 1913. The pastor, Fr. Syski (standing in the center with flowers on his jacket), was transferred to Hyde Park that month. Catherine Wos Dzioba (standing at the far right) holds her baby, who was born the previous December. Julia Kowaleski (wearing a ribbon and standing to Fr. Syski's right) was the chairwoman for this event.

THE KATA WEDDING. Franciszek (Frank) Kata had been living in Haverhill for a few years when he received word that a group of immigrants from his hometown of Nisko, Poland, had arrived in Pasaic, NJ. He went to Pasaic, met Agnes Wojdyla, married her, and brought her back to Haverhill. They had seven children and lived on Wilson Street. Frank and Agnes celebrated their 50th wedding anniversary in 1951. He died in 1959 and she died a year later.

JOSEPH WARCHOL. Joseph, a relative of the Katas, played a major role in the founding of St. Michael's Parish. He was treasurer of the original parish committee to raise funds. He also served on the 1908 committee that purchased the land where the church would be built. Joseph was born in 1873 and immigrated in 1903. He is shown with his son John and his daughter Rose.

THE RADULSKI WEDDING. The Radulski brothers were among the Polish pioneers in Haverhill. Adolf, the eldest, arrived in 1895 and was a major force behind the creation of St. Michael's Parish. Wincenty arrived in 1902, and Albin in 1908. There were also two other immigrant brothers, Julian and Konstanty, and a sister. The Radulskis came from Bialystock in Russian Poland. Albin (1886–1974) married Aniela Zwolak (1896–1948) in January 1914. Shown here are, from left to right, as follows: (front row) Adolf Radulski, Aniela, Albin, and Palagia (Zelska) Radulski (wife of Adolf); (back row) Wladyslawa Radulski (sister to Albin), Wincenty Radulski, Franciszka (Ryczko) Paszko, and Frank Zwolak (brother to Aniela).

MAGDALENA AND FRANCISZEK ANUSZEWSKI. Magdalena Wos (1881–1964) and her sister Tekla (1892–1965) immigrated about 1907 from Jezowie, Rzeszow, to join their sister, Catherine Wos Dziuba, in Haverhill. Frank Anuszewski (1883–1962), from Borowa, Rzeszow, came about the same year with his sister Antonina. Magdalena and Frank were married in the new St. Michael's Church on February 4, 1911, in the midst of a snowstorm. They had four children and lived on Chick Avenue.

96

ANNA SZELIGA. Anna (1894–1956) was born in Sojkowa, Galicia, in the Austrian part of Poland. She immigrated in 1909. According to the 1910 census she and her sister Sofia, who had immigrated in 1906, boarded at the house of George Adamcyk. Some time later that year, Sofia married Walenty Lesiczka. Both women were charter members of the Holy Rosary Society of St. Michael's Parish.

THE DRELICH WEDDING. Anna Szeliga married Antoni Drelich (1890–1953) in May of 1914. The wedding party included the following people, from left to right: (seated) an unidentified woman and Anna, Antoni, and Andrew Kots (1878–1972); (standing) Mary (Bayek) Januszewski, Wojciech Fila (1895–1940), Mary Tyburczy (1895–1980), Tomasj Kolodziej, and Sophie (Szeliga) Lesiczka.

ANTHONY WIECZERZAK, SCHOOLBOY. Tony was the son of Franciszek (1870–1950) and Tekla (Kurys) Wieczerzak (1879–1973). Both parents had immigrated in 1891. Frank went first to the coal mines in Pennsylvania and Tekla went to the textile mills of Lawrence. Tekla had come from the same village as Anna Szeliga. Tony was born in 1903. He is the blond schoolboy (right front) shown here with his classmates.

THE MOUNT WASHINGTON MARKET. Frank Wieczerzak operated a grocery store and butcher shop where his young son, Tony, worked after school and during vacations. That is Tony in his apron behind the meat counter. He continued to help his father run the store after he grew up. Tony died in 1997, aged 94. He divided his estate among various non-profit organizations including the Haverhill Public Library and the Haverhill Boys' Club.

THE PROCHNIEWICZ WEDDING PARTY. The lovely bride, Karalina Czerepak (1888–1970), wore a traditional Polish bridal wreath. Her groom, Maryan Prochniewicz (1888–1972), wore standard American attire. The members of the wedding party, from left to right, are s follows: (front row) Katherine Mandziej (1889–1965), Karolina, Maryan, and John Czerepak (1891–1976); (back row) unidentified, John Pazko, unidentified, John Wyka, and Mary Czerepak (1893–1982).

SADIE AND WOIJCIECH SZELIGA. Many familiar faces are in this wedding group. The groom, Woijciech or George, was the brother of Anna Drelich and Sofia Leciszka. Shown here, from left to right, are as follows: (front row) unidentified, Sadie (Kobylarz) Szeliga, George Szeliga, and Walenty and Sofia Lesiczka; (back row) Mary (Kobylarz) Byra, John Wyka, Mary Januszewski, and John Pazko.

MARY AND JOHN KATA. Both bride and groom immigrated to America in 1913. They married c. 1917. John Kata (1895–1970), the groom, was a shoe worker, and by 1920 the couple, plus their young son Joseph, were living at 8 Marble Street. All but the children in this photo have been identified. From left to right, they are as follows: (front row) Frances Rurak (1889–1974), Mary Kata (1895–1979), John Kata, and Wojciech Kots; (back row) Helen Pierog, Sophie (Wos) Bokszanski, Joseph Klecha, Fanny Bajek (d. 1980), and Joseph Wilk.

SOPHIE (WOS) BOKSZANSKI AND FREDDY. About the same time that she participated in the Kata wedding, Sophie Wos married Alphonse Bokszanski, an early immigrant who arrived in the states in 1900. Sophie came in 1910 to join her cousins, Tekla Wos and Magdalena (Wos) Anuskiewicz. Alphonse's first wife, Stefania, died at age 27 in September 1918 in the midst of the Great Flu Epidemic. Shown here with Sophie is Alphonse's son Freddy, who was born in 1914.

POLISH MUSICIANS. Alphonse Bokszanski (center), the husband of Sophie, played the accordion at various Polish picnics and parties. The violinist is John Sokolat (1890–1962), the second husband of Mary Rurak (p. 108). The gentleman on the left is remembered only as "Steve."

THE KLECHA WEDDING PARTY. More than any of the other groups portrayed in this book, members of the Polish community were likely to have kept wedding pictures, and many were offered for inclusion. Judging from the dress lengths and hair styles, this wedding probably occurred just after World War I. Shown here, from left to right, are as follows: (front row) Aniela (Klecha) Byra, Frances and Joseph Klecha, and unidentified. (back row) Sophie (Dzioba) Litwinowich (1897–1975), unidentified, unidentified, and John Wyka, who appears to have been everyone's favorite wedding usher.

MR. AND MRS. JOSEPH LESICZKA. A family with many siblings among the early immigrants from Poland were the Lesiczkas. Joseph and Mary Lesiczka were married about 1918. Shown here are, from left to right, as follows: (front row) Katherine, Sophie, Mary and Joseph Lesiczka (1886–1921), Joseph Palen (1889–1966), and Lena Lesiczka; (middle row) Tekla (1894–1983) and Joseph Wilk (1893–1951), unidentified, John Wyka, Josie Macul (1898–1981), and unidentified; (back row) Tekla Wos and Ignacy Lesiczka.

MR. AND MRS. IGNACY LESICZKA. Ignacy married about the same time that his brother Joseph did. Shown here, from left to right, are as follows: (front row) an unidentified child, Mary Sawick (1892–1968), Ignacy (1894–1932), Agnes Dziolo (1896–1995), and Walenty Lesiczka; (back row) unidentified, unidentified, Joseph Litwinovich, Tekla Wos, Ignace Pinkowski, and Sophie (Szeliga) Lesiczka.

SIMON AND MARY BOLENSKI. Simon had immigrated to America in 1903. He does not appear on the 1910 list of original parishioners of St. Michael's Church; however, he served many terms as president of the Polish National Alliance. Mary, his bride, was a 17-year-old immigrant in 1913. Mary is shown wearing a traditional myrtle-trimmed wedding veil. The Bolenskis' attendants were, from left to right, Agnes Lesiczka, Wladislaw Biernacki, Julius Kowaleski (p. 93), and Eva Rowinski (1895–1964).

JADWIGA AND WLADISLAW BIERNACKI. Wladislaw was a 35-year-old bachelor when the 1920 census was taken. He had immigrated in the early 1910s and served a number of terms with Simon Bolenski as an officer of the PNA. He married Jadwiga Kraus c. 1926. Her dress and cloche-style headdress reflect the drastic style changes of the Roaring Twenties.

THE JANUSZEWSKIS. Anthony Januszewski left a war-torn, but newly independent, Poland in 1919. He was 32 years old. His bride, Mary, had been 13 years old when she immigrated ten years before Anthony in 1909. They were married by the time of the 1920 census. Shown here, from left to right, are as follows: (front row) Anna Sasiela, Mary (Bayek) and Anthony Januszewski, and Frank Anuzewski; (back row) unidentified, John Grabiec (1896–1974), unidentified, and John Wyka.

MICHAEL TAUPEKA AND FRIEND. Michael (left) came to Haverhill from Poland in the 1920s. He held a variety of jobs in the shoe industry before becoming a salesman for the Smith Motor Co. As was typical of other unmarried young people of that time, he boarded with families until his marriage to Valeria Drelich (1908–1997) in the 1930s. Michael (1897–1965) was very active in various Polish men's organizations, including the Polish Home and the Pulaski Club. His friend has not been identified.

JOSEPH AND KATHERINE STETS. One of Michael Taupeka's closest friends after he immigrated to Haverhill was Joe Stets, a shoe worker. So it was fitting that when Joe (1894–1964) and Katherine Stets (1904–1985) (left) were married in the mid-1920s, Michael was the best man. Katherine wears a stylish cloche-style headdress. The lovely maid of honor has not been identified.

KSAWERY AND ALBINA ANTOLIEWICZ. Haverhill's Polish pioneers continued to welcome relatives from their home country through the 1920s. This young bride came to Haverhill to be with her Anuszewski aunt and uncle and married another recent immigrant. Shown here, from left to right, are as follows: (front row) Cousins Helen Wojtasiewicz and Mary and Stanley Anuszewski; (back row) Aunt Antoinette (Anuszewski) Wojtasiewicz (1885–1975), Uncle Frank Anuszewski, unidentified, unidentified, Lena Lesiczka, Joseph Golembicki, and Albina (1905–1957) and Ksawery (1896–1935) Antolewicz.

THE WYKA WEDDING. John Wyka (1893–1994) served as groomsman for countless of his friends throughout the 1910s and 1920s. Finally, his friends had the opportunity to attend his wedding. The wedding party included the following, from left to right: (front row) Carol ?, bride Franciszka Jarosz (1897–1985), John Wyka (1893–1994), and Woijciech/George Rurak (1889–1970); (back row) John's cousin, Mary Wicker (sic), Michael Bajek (d. 1961), unidentified, and John Grabiec.

A WAR VETERAN AND BRIDE. William Salas (1893–1971) served in the Polish Army in World War I and had the uniform to prove it. He married Natalia Leszczenska (1900–1970) in the early 1920s. The Salas' only son, Edmund, was killed in a plane crash in World War II. Katherine Kata, daughter of Frank and Agnes, is the third person in the back row. The others have not been identified.

MR. AND MRS. STANLEY WROBLESKI. Sophie Kowaleski, daughter of Julius and Julia, was born in 1900. She married Stanley Wrobleski (1893–1967) in January 1924. Her maid of honor (left) was her cousin, Sadie Suchodolski. The best man was Sophie's brother, Adam, a U.S. Marine. In August of that same year, Adam died of Bright's Disease. He was only 20 years old.

CHARLES AND KATHERINE SUPECK. Six months after her own marriage, Sophie (Kowaleski) Wrobleski served as an attendant at the marriage of her friend, Katherine Kata, to Charles Supeck from Marlboro, MA. The couple's attendants, standing from left to right behind them, are George Kots, Charles' unidentified sister, Tony Wojdyla, Veronica Wicko, John Warchol, and Sophie Wrobleski. Tragically, both Katherine Supeck and Sophie Wrobleski would die in the same year, 1933, just as they had wed in the same year. Katherine was 30 years old.

MARY RURAK SOKOLAT. Mary Stec immigrated to Haverhill in 1902 and married Andrew Rurak. They were charter members of St. Michael's Parish. The Ruraks already had three sons, Rudy, Joe, and Jake, when Andrew died in 1918 during the influenza epidemic. A fourth son, John (1919–1945), born after his father's death, was killed in World War II. Mary (1885–1963) then married John Sokolat (1890–1962) and they had a daughter, Annie. Mary Rurak Sokolat (left) and her son Joe are shown with Joe's mother-in-law, Julia Natyniak Zouris (1886–1965).

BASKETBALL CHAMPS. The Polish Young Men's Association won the city basketball championship in 1928. Shown here, from left to right, are as follows: (front row) Stanley Wysocki, Leon Lebor, and Joseph Rurak; (middle row) Joseph Koloshej/Cogge, William Wysocki, Walter "Budger" Wysocki, Jake Rurak, and Felix Andrus; (back row) Assistant Coach Charles Wasel, Charles Werzak, Joseph Warchol, and Coach Rudy Rurak. Bud Wysocki became the director of the Haverhill Boys' Club. Jake Rurak became a state senator, making him the first Pole to hold a major political office. Felix Andrus was a teacher and principal at Haverhill High School.

BASEBALL, TOO! The Polish Young Men's Association also sponsored a baseball team that made its mark on the local sports scene. These are the Wysocki brothers, Bill and Budger, and the year was 1929. They are probably at Swazey's Field, which was in the neighborhood of St. Michael's Church.

ADAM AND JOSEPHINE WYSOCKI. Adam Wysocki (1868–1956) and Josephine Kudla (1881–1959) arrived in America at the beginning of the 20th century. They settled into Lynn where their four sons—Stephen, Stanley, William, and Walter—were born. A daughter, Irene, was born after they moved to Haverhill. The Wysockis lived on Arch Street where they celebrated their 50th wedding anniversary in 1953. Pictured here, from left to right, are as follows: (front row) Josephine and Adam; (back row) Walter, William, Irene, Stephen, and Stanley.

THE KOSCIEWICZ FAMILY. Julius (1878–1937) and Anna Kosciewicz (1888–1948) first settled in Newport, NH. That is where their three children were born. In 1927, the family moved to Haverhill and opened a grocery store on Arch Street; later, they opened the White Eagle Market on Washington Street. The family eventually moved to Bradford and opened a second White Eagle Market on South Main Street. From left to right are Julius, Meacher/Mitchell (1908–1992), William (1910–1969), Appolonia/Pauline (1912–1986), and Anna.

DEDICATION OF THE POLISH HOME. For years, members of the Polish community had attempted to have a building that would serve as a cultural and social center. The building was completed in the midst of the Great Depression and formally dedicated in November 1936. Benny Fedenyszen (1918–1982), the 18-year-old leader of the Polish youth group "The Falcons," was sent to Poland to bring back soil from the homeland. At the dedication, the dirt was sprinkled on the small patch of lawn in front of the new Polish National Home. Benny is the young man in the Falcons uniform on the left of the second row.

Six

THE GREEKS

THE ZAHAROULIS FAMILY IN ASIA MINOR. The Zaharoulis family lived in Alatsata, Turkey—what ancient Greeks knew as Ionia. Shown here, from left to right, are as follows: (front) Sotiris; (middle row) George and Kiriakoole (Bitge) Zaharoulis, and grandmother Mary Rokkas (Kiriakoole's mother); (back row) Eothalia/Ethel, Theodore, Demosthenes, and Euthia. Theodore immigrated in 1912; his two sisters followed in 1914, and Sotiris immigrated in 1916. They originally went to Somerville where an older brother, John, lived. Ethel worked at Hood Rubber until she married Stephanos Bilmazes and moved to Haverhill.

THE BOUKIS FAMILY. The Boukis family came from Larrissa, Thessaly, north of Athens. This photograph was taken in 1910 after the older brothers, Nicholas (1887–1959) and Adam (1891–1956), left home for America. Nicholas went first, in 1907, then sent money for Adam to come in 1909. The two brothers brought their parents and sisters in 1913. Shown here are, from left to right, as follows: (front row) Euterpe (1903–), grandmother Stamatia Boukis, Michael (1858–1944), baby Eftie (1907–1996), and Eleni/Helen (1899–1987); (back row) Hariclea/Mary and mother Chrysoula (1861–1940).

PETER KATSURIBAS AND HIS PARENTS. Born in Megalopoly in the Peloponnesus in 1890, Peter was in Haverhill in time to be in the 1912 group of Greek Volunteers for the Balkans War. He married Fotina Gavostes (1890–1961) in Boston in 1914, and became an American citizen in 1919, when he and Fotina lived at 75 Temple Street. Peter's younger brother, John (1897–1988), also immigrated to Haverhill.

MILTIADES PANTELES AND FRIENDS. Miltiades (1888–1974, at right) had an adventurous early life. He came to Haverhill determined to learn English and not starve. He joined the army and went off to Texas to fight Pancho Villa. He did not starve, but he learned more Spanish than English. He returned to Haverhill and, in 1916, married Mirsine Coparan (1896–1996), sister of his best friend, Theodore. In 1920, he took his wife and daughter back to his home on the Isle of Lesvos, which had just been liberated from the Turks, and spent the decade fighting to liberate more areas. The other men in this picture have not been identified.

GLEKERIA AND DIONISIOS BRATIOTIS. This 1914 photograph shows Dionisios/Daniel (1883–1969) and his wife, Glekeria (1894–1988). In 1914 Dionisios was a shoe worker and the couple boarded at 24 Washington Avenue. In 1920, Dionisios is listed as owning a home at 75 Temple Street, where a George and a Louis Bratiotis also roomed. By 1941, the family lived at 15 Angle Street and children Christos, Mary, and Demetra were working, while daughter Cleopatra was a student.

HAVERHILL GREEK VOLUNTEERS. Greek immigrants in Haverhill and the region organized a military group to volunteer for the 1912–1913 Balkan War for the liberation of Northern Greece. They provided their own uniforms and rifles. The Poles and Italians also formed similar volunteer groups to aid their homelands. This photograph was taken at Winnekenni Castle by Kenoza Lake in Haverhill.

GEORGE KOSMES. George Kosmes, also known as Kosmas Papakosmas, was born in 1890 in Pantalofas, Macedonia, in northern Greece. Few Haverhill immigrants came from this area. George served in the U.S. Army in World War I. He married Kaliope (1894–1965) soon after the war ended and their first son, George, was born in 1920. George was a shoe worker with a house at 59 Primrose Street.

DIMOS DIMOPULOS. Dimos (1893–1961) came from Xiliki, Lamia, a village in central Greece near Thermopylae. He was in the Greek army in 1915 when this picture was taken. It is a Greek tradition that a man cannot marry until all of his sisters are wed. Calliope Tsangarakos from Athens was a younger sister. Her brother, who was in the Greek army, brought Dimos home for dinner to meet his sisters. He fell in love with the younger sister, but had to wait until 1922 to marry her.

THE DIMOPULOS BROTHERS. Three Dimopulos brothers came to Haverhill but only Dimos made it his permanent home. Shown here are, from left to right, Costa (the first to return to his home), George (a barber, the first to arrive in Haverhill, he returned to Greece with his wife Efstathia in the mid-1920s), and Dimos (who opened a custom tailor shop at the corner of Winter and Locust Streets). On his regular trips to Boston to purchase woolen cloth, Dimos also picked up paper products not only for his own store but for neighboring stores as well. He decided he would make more profit with the paper goods and opened the Star Paper Co. in 1922. His son-in-law, Nicholas (Katsuribas) Peterson, joined him in the business.

DIMOS AND CALLIOPE DIMOPULOS. Dimos had been in Haverhill for a few years when Calliope arrived to marry him. The ceremony took place in 1922, when this picture was taken. Dimos had a life-long concern for his home village. After his business became a success in Haverhill, he put much money into his ancestral home. He had a road to the nearest town opened, and had water piped into village. A stele was erected in his honor in the village.

EUMORPHIA DIMOPULOS. Eumorphia was the mother of the three Dimopulos brothers. She came to Haverhill and stayed until 1928, helping her daughter-in-law, Calliope, care for her two daughters. By the time she returned to her village of Xiliki, Lamie, her two sons, Costa and George, had already preceded her by a few years.

WILLIAM LOUCOPOULOUS AND HIS CHILDREN. The Loucopoulus family lived on Lewis Street, Cedar Street, and eventually, 89 Broadway. William, or Vasilios, was born in 1874. His wife, Sirmou, or Mary, was born in 1885 and died in 1969. They were married early in the 20th century. Shown here, from left to right, are as follows: (seated) William (1874–1946); (back row) daughter Jenny (1905–1973, wearing a costume from Lamie) and sons Peter (1912–1943), George (1909–1964), and William. Peter and his younger brother, Charles (1923–1944), were both killed in World War II—one of only two pair of brothers from the city to give their lives in the conflict.

STEPHEN AND ETHEL BILMAZES. Stephanos Bilmazes, born in 1886, left the port of Piraeus, Greece, aboard the SS *Neustria* for America in 1907. His first destination was Somerville, but he was in Haverhill by 1916. That is the year he returned to Somerville to marry Euthia/Ethel Zaharoulis (p. 111). Both bride and groom came from Alatzata, Turkey. Stephen had a grocery store at 84 Water Street and the family lived above the store. The Bilmazes had three children—Orestes (1917–1921), Virginia, and Electra. Stephen died in 1962 and Ethel died in 1965.

A Lesvos Picnic, 1918. This photograph of a group of immigrants from the Isle of Lesvos is a microcosm of Greek immigration to Haverhill, as it is disproportionately male. Females came in family groups or because of an arranged marriage. It was very rare for a Greek woman to immigrate on her own or to work outside the home. One result was a large number of Greek male immigrants among the first generation who remained life-long bachelors because of the unavailability of marriageable women. The men would work in the shoe shops and share rooms. One of the men would be designated to handle the shopping, cooking, and cleaning. This lifestyle explains the great need for, and popularity of, coffeehouses. Among the surnames in this group picture are Miserlis, Pananos, Tickelis, and Zavaglos. The older woman seated with the baby in the front at left is Irene Zavaglos' mother (p. 123).

A LESVOS REUNION, 1922. Four years after the previous picnic, the Lesvos immigrants had many more young families, indicating the growing Greek community. In addition to the names mentioned on p. 118, other Lesvos immigrants included the Demerges, Alexanders, Kamberoules, Dekeons, Vataseous, Papoutsys, Savos, Bousnakis, Theofilis, Karekos, Patrakos, and Capetanelis families.

GIRLS AT THE BEACH. Posing here, from left to right, are as follows: (front row) Stasia and Dorothy Coparan; (back row) Euterpe, Helen, and Eftie Boukis, and Calliope Dimitrouli. Euterpe Boukis became the first Haverhill Greek woman to graduate from college. She married a classmate, Dr. Panos Dukakis, and is the mother of former Massachusetts Gov. Michael Dukakis, the 1988 Democratic presidential nominee. Helen (1888–1974) married Theodore Coparan; Eftie never married. Calliope Dimitrouli was a cousin of Theodore Coparan.

119

A LIBERTY BOND PARADE. When the United States entered World War I on the side of the Allies, all of its immigrants responded to the call. Four Greek men—Peter Kaloumiris, Vasilios Sileris, Christos Starvis, and George Verdoukos—died in the war. The Greeks also responded to the Liberty Bond Drives that were held. This parade, with its Hellenic theme, passed the second church used by the Greeks. It was a former Advent church on Walnut Street and was used for Orthodox religious services for 30 years, until it was replaced by the current Holy Apostles Church on Winter Street.

A LIBERTY BOND PARADE, PART II. In this photograph, the parade has passed the Greek church on Walnut Street and is approaching Emerson Street. The floats in this photograph had patriotic themes with the flags of the Allies, and the children were in uniforms. The sign barely visible in the back reads in part: ". . . Greeks Fighting . . ." The driver of the front van resembles Dr. Constantine Popoff, a Bulgarian, who ministered to the Greeks in Haverhill.

THE ZOUKIS FAMILY. Mehael/Michael (1864–1941) and Areka/Rita (1872–1955) Zoukis, seated in the center, and their four sons immigrated from Northern Macedonia to Haverhill in 1912. Sotiris (1903–1921, at far left) died of rheumatic fever while in high school. Nicholas (1901–1995, center left) opened The Fruit Basket in Bradford in 1927. He added a soda fountain in 1934 and made the store a favorite gathering spot. George (1896–1959, center right) went from being a shoe cutter to being a foreman for George Valhouli's Lincoln Shoe. John (1899–1987, at far right) was a tailor with Gerros Men's Shop before joining Nick at The Fruit Basket in 1944.

THOMAS AND MARY PAPACHRISTON. Thomas Papachriston (1888–1926) was born in Macedonia but moved to Turkey. His first wife died in childbirth along with her baby. Thomas came to America where he met and wed Mary Liguros (1897–1937) c. 1918. The beautiful Mary wore a lovely veil. Thomas was a shoe worker and the couple had three children.

A PICNIC AT THE GIANOPOULOS FARM. There were about 1,700 Greeks living in Haverhill by 1930. A great majority of them lived in the area around Winter, Primrose, and Harrison Streets that the Irish had dubbed "The Acre." Some, however, chose the countryside. Christos Gianopoulos had a farm off of Salem Street, Bradford, that was a great gathering spot in warm weather for his clansmen from central Greece. This photograph was taken about 1924. Shown here, from left to right, are as follows: (first row) Katherine Stanford, Foula Dimopulos, Emmanuel and Theodore Gianopoulos, and unidentified; (second row) Eumorphia and Calliope Dimopulos, Helen Deros, Efstathia Dimopulos, and Mrs. Christos Gianopoulos; (third row) Bacilios and Triada Bougioukas, Katherine and Georgette Gianopoulos, unidentified, and Thea Sanford; (fourth row) Savas Deros, George Dimopulos, Christos Gianopoulos, unidentified, and James Sanford, who was born in Salonika. The next four are not identified.

LEADERS OF GREEK SOCIETY. Irene Zervoglos (1897–1971) was considered the "grande dame" of Greek society. Her husband, George (1892–1969), operated the New England Shoe Trimming Co. and served for many years as president of the Greek community. Mirsine (Coparan) Panteles was the wife of Miltiades (p. 113) and her brother, Theodore Coparan, was a shoe manufacturer. She and Irene were from the Isle of Lesvos. Cleona Zazopoulos (1893–1997) was from Pontus on the Black Sea, a part of the Russian Empire. Her husband, Christos (1884–1964), was a founder of the Radio Market on Walnut Street.

THOMAS PAPACHRISTON AND HIS CHILDREN. Thomas and his three children are shown in the yard of their home on Kimball Street. He is holding his young son, Arthur (1925–1996). His girls are Nina (b. 1921, standing in front) and Laura (b. 1919). Arthur served for many years as head of the Haverhill Board of Health. Thomas Papachriston died soon after this picture was taken at the age of 38.

SOTIRIS ZAHAROOLIS (1902–1972).
Soter (p. 111) was the last of his family to come to America. He arrived in 1916 and lived in Haverhill with his sister Ethel and her husband, Stephen Bilmazes. Soter graduated from Haverhill High in 1922 and attended Mt. Hermon prep school. He went to Tufts University Medical School and was city physician for the city of Somerville for many years. He is shown here outside his brother-in-law's store on Water Street where he worked while in school.

THE TICKELIS BROTHERS. James (1889–1976) and John (1894–1972), along with their brother Stavros, came from the Isle of Lesvos. James was the owner of Martin and Tikellis (sic) Shoe Factory, which was started in Ipswich and then moved to Newburyport. John was a partner in General Shoe and Leather, 18 Granite Street. This picture dates from 1927. Posing here are, from left to right, James, with his son Ignatius; James' wife, Nifodora (Fronia Papoutsy, 1903–1976); John's wife, Chrisa Smyrniou (1897–1996); and John, with his daughter Ourania, who would marry Arthur Papachriston.

LUCY AND NICHOLAS MANGOURANIS. Lucy was born in Skalohorion, Lesvos, in 1912. Her father immigrated in 1911, just before Lucy was born. Soon after Lucy's birth, her mother, with her other children, left to join her husband. The decision was made to leave Lucy with her paternal grandparents to ease their loneliness. It was not until 1924, after her grandparents died, that Lucy was reunited with her parents. She is shown with her father soon after her arrival in Haverhill.

THE PANANOS FAMILY. Lucy Mangouranis (1912–1974) married fellow Lesvos immigrant Nicholas Pananos (1894–1961) in the early 1930s. Nicholas was a shoe worker and a celebrated cook. This photograph was taken in the summer of 1937 and shows Nicholas and Lucy with their three daughters, Frances, Anna, and Mary Ann (in her mother's arms). The family home was at 64 Harrison Street.

THE KATSURIBAS FAMILY. Fatine (Govostes) Katsuribas (1890–1961) and her husband, Peter (1890–1980), are shown with their two sons, Nicholas and William. In the 1920s, Peter is listed as owning the Lexington Spa. By 1940, he was a shoe worker and from that date on the family home was 272 Washington Street. Peter was an active member of the Greek community. He served on the fund-raising committee for a new church. Both Peter and Nicholas (better known as Nicholas Peterson) served as presidents of the Greek community. Both of the Katsirubas boys were highly decorated veterans of World War II—Nicholas in the U.S. Army Air Corps and William in the U.S. Navy.

"CHARLEY BAKER." Constantinos Vlahakis (1889–1971) immigrated from Karpenisi, near Lamia, in 1907 to New York City. He returned to Greece in 1912 to fight the Turks. He married his wife, Evangelia (1893–1966), from Ayrion, Yeoryos, in 1914 but could not bring her to join him in Haverhill until 1921. Constantinos was a baker and cook. He worked for Colonial Lunch and Thompson's Bakery, among others. To many people he was known as "Charley Baker." The family lived at 69 Harrison Street in the Acre.

Miss Eliades, Greek Tutor.

Phontine Eliades was a private tutor in Greek, but not a teacher in the official Greek school on Locust Street. Students went to her if they wished to have a proper Athenian accent. She never married, and was very proud of her single status. In the 1941 City Directory she is listed as boarding with James Patterson, 303 Broadway, the proprietor of Patterson's Tea Room. She returned to Athens upon her retirement, where this photograph was taken in 1968.

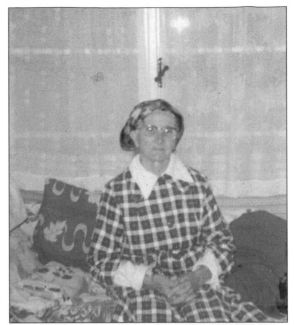

The Zoukis Wedding. Nicholas Zoukis (1901–1995) married American-born Laura Papachriston (1919–) in August 1937. Shown here, from left to right, are as follows: (front row) Irene Pispeickas, Michael Zouke, and Rita Zouke; (middle row) Michael James, Athena Kostas, Nicholas, Laura, Nina Papachriston, and Charlotte Zouke; (back row) Michael James Sr. Laura's mother, Mary Papachriston, died a few months after the wedding.

GEORGE VALHOULI. George was born in 1894 in Samarina, Macedonia, Greece. Few Greeks from Macedonia settled in Haverhill. They primarily settled in Nashua and Manchester, NH. He and his father came to Haverhill when George was 12, to work in the shoe shops and earn money. When his father decided to return home, George chose to stay in Haverhill. He served in the American Army during World War I. Upon returning from the war, he learned the shoe business and established the Lincoln Shoe Company. His shoe company was a source of regular employment for new immigrants for decades. There is a fitting tribute on George's cemetery marker: "If you were hungry he gave you food. If you were thirsty he gave you drink. If you needed work, he gave you work." After World War II and the devastation of the Greek Civil War, he brought over Koula Valhouli, widow of his late brother Nicholas, and her five sons—John, Peter, Michael, Archimedes, and James. This photograph was taken in 1935, when George (center) was visiting his home town. He is shown with a friend, and with the uncle of his wife, Fanny, a Mr. Spanos, who is dressed in traditional clothes. George died in 1974.